THE FASHION INDUSTRY DOESN'T WANT YOU TO READ THIS BOOK

by Jonathan Ohayon

Copyright © 2024 by Jonathan Ohayon

All rights reserved.

No part of this book may be reproduced in any form or by any electronic or mechanical means, including information storage and retrieval systems, without written permission from the author, except for the use of brief quotations in a book review.

Because of the dynamic nature of the Internet, any web addresses or links contained in this book may have changed since publication and may no longer be valid.

For any questions please use the 'contact us' page from fakemovement.com or email us at info@fakemovement.com

ISBN Amazon Paperback: 979-8-325-03376-6
ISBN: 979-8-218-40892-3
Imprint: F.A.K.E. Movement

I dedicate this book to honor the humans and animals whose lives were unjustly taken by the fashion industry.

Table Of Contents

About the author 11
Introduction 15

WHAT IS FASHION? 19

What is Fashion, and who created it? 21
What is Sustainable Fashion? 23
What is Vegan Fashion? 26
What is Minimal Fashion? 28
What is inclusive Fashion? 29
What is circular (or regenerative) Fashion? 30
What is "Zero-waste" in Fashion? 32
Fast Fashion VS Slow Fashion, what's the difference? 34
What is Greenwashing? 36
Retro vs vintage, what's the difference? 41
What does "Transparent" mean in fashion? 42

TEXTILE and its environmental impact 45

Natural or Organic clothing, what's the difference? 47
Cotton or organic cotton, what's the difference? 49
Is bamboo fabric ecological? *Rayon, Viscose, Lyocell,
Tencell, and Linen... What's the difference?* 54
Is hemp the solution of tomorrow? 57
Is linen the solution of tomorrow? 59
PU fabric or PVC, what's the difference? 61
Fabrics: Which one has the worst environmental impact? 63

ANIMALS in fashion 67

Is leather a by-product of the meat industry? 69
Chemicals - Which ones are used to create leather? 71
What is Chromium? 80
Is vegetable tanning / veg-tan of animal leather
an ethical and ecological solution? 82
Pee in leather? 85

Plastic in leather? 87
What is genuine leather? 89
Cat and dog leather... Does it really exist? 90
Kangaroo leather? 93
Exotic leather, how luxurious it is? 95
Human leather... Really? 97
Is wool ethical? 99
Alpaca fiber, is it ethical? 102
What is cashmere? Is it ethical? 104
Rats in my clothes? 106
Down, is it ethical? 107
Why silk is so bad for the planet? 109
Are pearls ethical? 111
Fur will soon be banned worldwide, why not leather? 113
Second-hand leather, is it considered Vegan? 116
Animal welfare in fashion, what is it? 117

HUMANS in fashion 121

What is a "sweatshop"? 123
What is "Rana Plaza" and what happened there? 125
What does "handmade" means? 127
Is the "minimum wage" ethical? 129
Modern slavery, is it really present in the fashion industry? .. 131
"The fashion industry exploits children", is it true? 132
What is MICA? And why is it so bad? 134
Is it possible to be a feminist and buy fast fashion? 136
Boycotting fast fashion, do workers suffer from it? 139
What diseases "toxic" clothing can cause? 141
How can your body absorb chemicals
from "toxic" clothing? 142
Is wearing clothes also wearing values? 143
Does buying new clothes make us happy? 144
Could fashion have an impact on our mental health? 147

PRODUCTION and its environmental impact 153

How many clothes are made each year? 155
Is 'made in Europe' or 'made in USA' necessarily ethical? 157

$9.99 T-shirt, how is this price possible? 159
Luxury fashion, does expensive necessarily mean ethical? 161
What happens to unsold clothes? 163
Is vegan fashion necessarily ethical,
ecological, and responsible? 165
Microplastic, how much is released into the oceans
by the fashion industry? 166
Water, how much is wasted by the fashion industry? 168
Is it ethical to donate your clothes? 171

SOLUTIONS 177

What to do with your old clothes? 179
What is sustainable packaging? 181
Washing | How to take care of your clothes
in an ethical way? 182
How to find a responsible wedding dress? 184
Is buying a Halloween costume ethical? 185
What if unisex fashion was the solution? 186
What are the alternatives to animal "products"? 187
How to really support vegan and ethical brands? 190
How can we be sure that a brand is truly ethical? 191
Consumers or brands, who has the power? 193
Is vegan fashion just a passing trend? 194
Is 3D design a good solution? 195
And now? 197
A good place to start. 200

Sources 203

About the author

Jonathan Ohayon, a passionate entrepreneur and animal rights activist, who has made it his mission to create a more ethical fashion industry.

Growing up in Paris, France, Jonathan was deeply influenced by his family's rich heritage in the fashion industry. From his grandparents, who were both skilled tailors, to his father, a retailer of fashion accessorie,,s, fashion and entrepreneurship were integral parts of his childhood. By the age of 6, Jonathan was already assisting his father at local markets!

His journey took a significant turn in 2014 when he adopted veganism, driven by a deep commitment to ethical principles. A year later, he co-founded Arsayo alongside his father and brother. Initially recognized for their innovative secured city backpack, which garnered awards from the prestigious Lepine contest and the French Ministry of Interior, the company has since expanded its mission. Arsayo now crafts vegan and ethically made backpacks and accessories, utilizing innovative, sustainable alternatives to animal leather.

Jonathan is also an animal rights activist, frequently participating in animal liberation demonstrations in Los Angeles, where he now lives. In 2019, he founded the F.A.K.E movement, that aims to elevate vegan fashion by creating pop-up events in iconic cities such as Los Angeles, Paris, and Tel Aviv.

"The F.A.K.E. Movement [Fashion for Animal Kingdom & Environment] was created out of necessity" said Jonathan. After a couple years living in Los Angeles, Jonathan couldn't find any places to showcase the Arsayo brand that were both vegan and ethically made. This is why he decided to create a pop-up event where brands could proudly display their products, knowing that everything around them was aligned with their values.

The popup were such a success that Jonathan decided it wasn't enough. He then created the very first Vegan Fashion Museum in the middle of Los Angeles.

His work has been recognized by some of the world's most prestigious publications, including Vogue, the New York Times, and LA Times. In 2023, Jonathan Ohayon received a certificate of recognition from the city of West Hollywood for serving the community as a speaker to bring more awareness to environmental issues.

Jonathan recently developed an online marketplace dedicated to vegan and ethically made fashion. **Fakemovement.com** serves as a testament to his commitment to making sustainable and cruelty-free fashion accessible to a broader audience.

Check the website and learn about vegan and ethical fashion with podcasts, blog articles, new innovatives products. Subscribe to their newsletter to learn more!

Now, after three years in the making, Jonathan has released his latest project, a book aimed to educate consumers and helping people understand what ethical fashion truly is and how they can avoid falling into the greenwashing trap.

This book is designed for anyone who is interested in fashion, including enthusiasts, designers, students, social, environmental, and animal rights activists.

"The Fashion Industry Doesn't Want You To Read This Book" is a must-read!

*"You are a super hero and your super power is choice!
Choose wisely"*

Jonathan Ohayon

Introduction

The goal of this book is not to make you an ethical and sustainable fashion expert, but to open your eyes, mind, and heart to the deepest secrets of the fashion industry.

There are over 70 questions on multiple topics, from the different terms in the fashion industry to the different fabric and their impact on the environment, as well as the different practices that impact human life and animals. Each of these topics could be the subject of a whole book, and it was a long and exhausting process of research and rewriting to condense them all into one book.

VERY IMPORTANT: Please, do not feel judged while reading this book!!!

I will never say it enough. Even if you realize in this book that your choices impacted human working conditions, the animals, or the environment, **this is not YOUR fault!**

First of all, you were probably unaware of the impact of your fashion choices. The fashion industry is very good at keeping its secret and playing tricks with our brain to making us buy whatever they want. Because yes, most of the purchases we make in the fashion industry aren't for us, but for others... or how we appear to others.

Secondly, you are not the ultimate decision-maker of the brand you bought.

After reading some parts, you might feel overwhelmed and will be deciding to never wear any clothes again, but please believe the intention of this book is NOT to judge you.

This book is not your enemy, it is your honest friend.

The one who will tell you straight forward in your eyes what are the consequence of your fashion choices and make sure that you understand the ramifications of it.

The goal of "The Fashion Industry Doesn't Want You To Read This Book" is to open your eyes and help you take **the red pill of the fashion industry matrix** to better understand your choices.

Hopefully, after this book, you will be more in line with your values and will make better fashion choices. Not only for the planet, the animals, and the humans.. but for you!

This book is made to be very easy to understand, and it only touch the tip of the iceberg of every topic. I deeply encourage you to do more research if one of the questions resonates with you. If this happened, then this book would have completed its mission!

WHAT IS FASHION?

What is Fashion, and who created it?

Fashion is something that we deal with every day of our life. Even people who say they don't care what they wear choose clothes every morning that say a lot about them and how they feel that day.

Fashion is often seen as a way to express ourselves. It can also be considered a business that predicts our clothing choices and how we want to appear to others. But Fashion is more than just a business; it is also a social and cultural phenomenon that connects to our values and core beliefs.

Pinpointing the origin of Fashion is challenging, as it has developed over time and been impacted by cultural and historical influences. Different regions and periods have their own unique fashion styles, and these styles have often been influenced by the materials and techniques available, as well as the social and cultural norms of the time.

Clothing has been a part of human history for thousands of years. The exact date when humans first started wearing clothes is unknown, but evidence of clothing dates back at least 120,000 years[1]. The first clothes were likely used for warmth and protection from the elements.

As human societies became more complex, clothing began to serve additional purposes and started to be used to indicate social status, to express cultural identity and to display personal style. The development of textiles and weaving techniques allowed for greater variety and complexity in clothing design.

To the modern days, there is a common perception that the Fashion culture was initiated in 1826 by Charles

Frederick Worth[2] in Paris, known as "the father of haute couture" and the first Fashion designer as we understand it today.

In this book, we will explore how **fashion can be used as a tool for positive change** in the world.

"Fashion is not something that exists in dresses only. Fashion is in the sky, in the street, fashion has to do with ideas, the way we live, what is happening."

- Coco Chanel

What is Sustainable Fashion?

Sustainability is a concept that has been around for centuries, but it wasn't until the 1980s that it became the buzzword we all know and love. The modern definition of sustainability emerged during this time, when the United Nations' Brundtland Commission released their report "Our Common Future" in 1987[1]. The report defined sustainable development as **"meeting the needs of the present without compromising future generations' ability to meet their own needs."**

It's important to acknowledge that while the Brundtland Commission played a significant role in making sustainability a frequently discussed topic, **the concept itself has its roots in traditional and indigenous knowledge systems.** These systems have long recognized the importance of preserving resources for future generations and living in harmony with nature. As such, it's difficult to attribute the creation of sustainability to any one person or group. Instead, it's a concept that has evolved over time, shaped by different cultures and ideas.

Sustainable fashion has taken off, and it's no surprise. The fashion industry is a major contributor to global waste and pollution, and they need to take action.

Sustainable fashion is all about designing, producing, and thoughtfully selling clothing, footwear, and accessories with a focus on environmental protection, ethical practices, and social responsibility. Often misunderstood, sustainable fashion isn't just about taking care of our planet by choosing eco-friendly materials. It is a combination ethical production, conscious consumption, and long-term durability.

The concept of sustainable fashion is built on three pillars:

- **Environmental sustainability** involves reducing the environmental impact of the fashion industry by using materials and methods that minimize pollution and waste. This includes using renewable and biodegradable materials, reducing water and energy use, and promoting closed-loop production processes where waste is reduced, and resources are conserved.

- **Social sustainability** focuses on the ethical treatment of workers and communities involved in the production of fashion items. This includes fair labor practices, safe working conditions, and the promotion of cultural diversity. It also means ensuring that the products are made without exploiting people or communities and that workers receive fair wages and benefits.

- **Economic sustainability** involves ensuring that the fashion industry is economically viable, both for the companies and for the consumers. This means that fashion items should be priced in a way that reflects the true cost of production, and that companies should have sustainable business practices that promote long-term viability. This also means that consumers should be educated on the importance of sustainable fashion and be able to access products that are both environmentally and socially responsible, as well as affordable.

Sustainable fashion also involves consumers being mindful of their own purchasing habits and considering the impact of their fashion choices on the environment and communities. Additionally, it can involve supporting and promoting brands that prioritize sustainability and transparency in their supply chains.

Sustainable fashion offers a way to address the environmental and social issues posed by the fashion industry. By focusing on the three pillars of sustainability: environmental, social, and economic.

FACT

In order to be Sustainable, a Fashion item MUST compass these three pillars:

Environmental
Social
Economic

What is Vegan Fashion?

Vegan fashion is a term used to describe clothing, footwear, and accessories that are made without the use of any animal products. This means that materials like leather, silk, wool, feathers, and others that are derived from animals are not used in the production of these items. With growing consumer awareness of the ethical and environmental impacts of fashion, vegan fashion has become a popular choice.

While vegan fashion eliminates the exploitation of animals in the production of clothing, it's important to note that not all vegan products are sustainable. Some vegan clothing may still be made using synthetic materials that are not biodegradable or produced using toxic dyes that can harm the environment. Additionally, in the fast-fashion industry, some workers involved in the production of clothing (that may technically be considered vegan) may not be paid fairly or at all.

Vegan fashion is all about saying "no" to animal products, sustainable fashion is about taking the fashion industry to the next level. It's not just about being kind to animals, it's about being kind to the planet and all the people involved in its creation. Sustainable fashion aims to minimize its environmental footprint and make the fashion world a fairer place for all. This means using environmentally friendly methods in production, such as using biodegradable materials, and ensuring that workers are paid fairly and treated ethically.

In this book, we will dive deep into the environmental impact of animal products used in the fashion industry. We will see that animal-derived materials, such as leather and wool, have a much greater impact on the environment than vegan alternatives (even synthetic materials)[1]. The production of animal products requires large amounts of land, water, energy, and contributes to deforestation, greenhouse gas emissions, and other environmental problems.

We will as well reveal practices that can be disturbing. However, it is important to acknowledge them and understand that to have an animal "product" we need an animal.

While vegan fashion is a step in the right direction, it's not always sustainable. However, sustainable fashion should always be vegan as it supports an ethical and environmentally responsible fashion industry.

FACT

Vegan fashion is not always sustainable, but sustainable fashion should always be vegan.

What is Minimal Fashion?

Minimal fashion is all about simplicity, quality, and sustainability. It's about investing in classic pieces that will last for years rather than filling your closet with trendy items that will end up in a landfill after a few wears.

Minimal fashion focuses on essential pieces that can be mixed and matched to create countless outfits.

Think classic organic t-shirts, high-quality sustainable jeans, and versatile jackets that can be dressed up or down.

But minimal fashion is not just about the clothes. It's about the mindset. It's about recognizing the impact that the fashion industry has on the environment and choosing to make a difference. It's about making conscious decisions and choosing quality over quantity.

So because we know (especially after reading this book) the harmful and dangerous impact of fast fashion and overconsumption, what if we tried for once, or every time, or when we can, to ask ourselves if "this" extra thing, **we really need it?**

Who knows, you might just love the freedom and versatility of a minimalist wardrobe.

What is inclusive Fashion?

Inclusive fashion is when fashion is accessible and represents everyone! The fashion industry has always established boundaries between ethnicities, genders, sexual orientations, beauty ideals, body proportions, or status...

Inclusive fashion is the exact opposite; it's fashion that "includes" everyone.

In short, inclusive fashion is the fashion of tomorrow today! The one that breaks these boundaries involves everyone, all diversity, all social, cultural, or financial backgrounds... to promote equality, share love, strengthen ties, and promote understanding.

Even fashion brands can benefit from inclusive fashion!

By embracing diversity and catering to a wider range of customers, fashion brands can tap into new markets and expand their reach. This can lead to increased revenue and brand loyalty, as customers feel seen and valued by the fashion industry.

Additionally, **promoting inclusivity in fashion can have a positive social and cultural impact by promoting acceptance, respect, and understanding of diverse identities and experiences.**

What is circular (or regenerative) Fashion?

We are the only species on earth that creates trash. The so-called circular or regenerative fashion is a fashion that aims to destroy the infernal cycle of "buy - wear - throw away" of fast fashion.

To destroy this vicious cycle, circular fashion imagines more thoughtful clothing, directly created with "a possible next use" in mind.

In regenerative fashion, everything is taken into account! From the choice of the raw material used to the design, nothing is left to chance; everything is thought to be transformed afterward (into another garment or a totally different product).

Circular fashion is all about "the afterlife of our clothes" by directly creating clothes that won't become waste later on.

By embracing a **closed-loop system**, the fashion industry could achieve a sustainable approach where materials are continually reused and recycled, resulting in reduced waste and pollution. This would limit the reliance on virgin raw materials, promote the regeneration of natural systems, and decrease textile waste.

Fashion's current linear model requires significant overhaul, and the adoption of circularity could provide a solution. A circular system has the potential to address crucial challenges faced by the global fashion industry, such as climate change, pollution, and waste. Additionally, it could create opportunities for responsible growth.

To enable a circular fashion, products must meet certain

criteria, although there is currently no agreed-upon definition or industry standard. Specifically, products need to:
- Be designed for long-term use
- Be made to be remade
- Use safe, recycled, or renewable materials

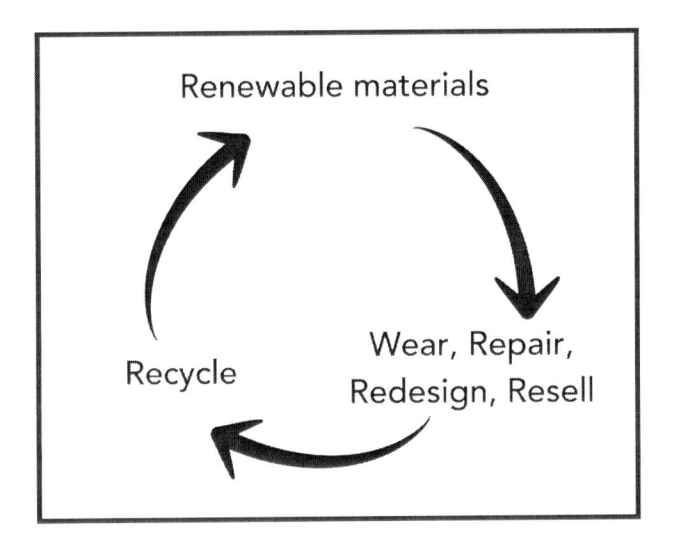

Renewable materials

Recycle

Wear, Repair, Redesign, Resell

What is "Zero-waste" in Fashion?

The idea of zero waste in fashion is literally... to avoid any process that promotes the creation of waste.

In the zero-waste fashion, we distinguish two main categories into which the associations and companies put all their efforts.

Zero waste "pre-customer" - that is to say, to make sure that the creation of a product (before the customer has it in hand) produces no waste. For example, designers can think about how to cut garments from fabrics so that all the raw material is optimized and used.

And then there's **"post customer" zero waste** - that is, trying to limit waste once the customer is "done" using the product (or fed up with that old T-shirt). Solutions include mass awareness campaigns and the "3R" approach of reducing, reusing, and recycling products.

Although zero-waste fashion is not a new concept, the fast fashion industry poses challenges to its implementation. However, every little action counts, and collective awareness is a crucial first step toward a more sustainable fashion industry. There are many examples of successful zero-waste practices in the fashion industry, such as :

- **"Closed-loop" manufacturing**, where waste from production is collected, sorted, and reused in the production process..
- **Sustainable material sourcing**, prioritizing the use of sustainable and renewable materials in the product, such as organic or recycled fabrics.
- **"Upcycling" and "Remaking"**, from waste materials or using existing clothing to create new

designs.
- **Circular economy models**, where products are designed for long-term use and materials are continually reused and recycled.
- **Sustainable packaging**, to reduce waste from shipping and delivery.

These are just a few examples of successful zero-waste practices in the fashion industry. As awareness grows and technology advances, we can expect to see more innovative solutions to reduce waste and promote sustainability in fashion.

It is essential to focus on these positive developments and the progress being made towards a more environmentally friendly fashion industry.

Overall, zero-waste fashion is an optimistic movement that encourages manufacturers and consumers alike to make sustainable choices and reduce waste in the fashion industry.

Fast Fashion VS Slow Fashion, what's the difference?

The Fashion Industry is a complex and dynamic sector, with two contrasting approaches that dominate the market: Fast Fashion and Slow Fashion.

Fast Fashion *(the villain)* is characterized by **high-speed production, excessive consumption, and waste.** This model prioritizes profits over people and the environment, leading to the exploitation of workers, environmental degradation, and manipulation of consumers. In this system, everyone loses, from the workers who suffer in inhumane working conditions, to the consumers who are constantly bombarded with an ever-increasing stream of products and pressure to keep up with the latest trends.

In stark contrast, Slow Fashion *(the superhero)* advocates for **conscious consumption and sustainable production.** Slow Fashion focuses on producing only what is necessary, using environmentally friendly materials and processes, and ensuring fair labor practices. This approach prioritizes the well-being of the workers, the environment, and the consumers.

When we adopt Slow Fashion, we take control of our own wants and needs, and empower ourselves to make a positive impact on the world around us.

Fast fashion contributes to the planet's ecosystem degradation due to its voracious resource use, the short lifespan of its products, and the considerable pollution generated throughout manufacturing. In comparison, Slow Fashion emphasizes the use of natural fibers and eco-friendly materials, reducing the overall harm to the environment.

In conclusion, it's time to acknowledge the harmful consequences of Fast Fashion and make a conscious effort to embrace Slow Fashion. By making this shift, we can help create a fairer, greener, and more sustainable world for all.

It's time to realize that we are also victims, fooled by abusive marketing, and that buying, or rather not buying, is a power we all have every day to make things change, to stop (or at least to slow down) the infernal machine.

What is Greenwashing?

How to write a book on ethical and sustainable fashion without addressing the issue of greenwashing; this unethical practice used by marketers who abuse our trust to sell more.

Like a soft lie, an embellished truth, a transformed message, an improved speech... greenwashing is when a brand, a company, a group, or a product claim to be "green" or "responsible" without really being so, only by playing on marketing and communication.

Food, automotive, political, technological, textile, cosmetic... Greenwashing exists in all consumer sectors, and poorly sanctioned (if sanctioned), it is an unfortunately fruitful practice that is not ready to stop.

In fact, greenwashing's goal are essentially the same goals that the fast fashion industry has, to make you believe in a beautiful lie. A beautiful lie that tells you that you need more, and you need it more often (fast fashion), and that is achieved by thousands of ads with pretty words and catchphrases to sell you that lie (greenwashing), and just because it's pretty and cheap and easy, you believe in it.

To help consumers identify such practices, environmental marketing agency TerraChoice developed the "six sins of greenwashing."[1]

Sin #1: Hidden Trade-Off.

This is like a wolf in sheep's clothing, where companies focus on one positive aspect of their product while ignoring the negative ones. **Example:** A clothing company claims to be eco-friendly because they use organic cotton. However, they neglect to mention the heavy use of synthetic dyes that release toxic chemicals into water sources during production.

Sin #2: No Proof.

This is like a magician's trick, where companies make environmental claims without any evidence to back them up. **Example:** A fashion brand claims its products are made with sustainable materials, but they have nothing to offer when asked for certification or documentation.

Sin #3: Vagueness.

This is like a game of charades where companies use vague and ambiguous terms to make their product seem environmentally friendly. **Example:** A fashion brand labels its products as "sustainable fashion" but provides no specific information about its environmental practices or materials used in production.

Sin #4: Irrelevance.

This is like a trojan horse, where companies make technically true environmental claims that are not significant to the product's actual environmental impact. **Example:** A brand could claim to be "fur-free," when fur has been banned and the product may still contain other animal products.

Sin #5: Fibbing.

This is like a fake ID, where companies use irrelevant or deceptive labels to trick consumers into thinking their product is environmentally friendly. **Example:** A company could create their own "Eco-friendly Certified" label without any real criteria or third-party verification.

Sin #6: Lesser of Two Evils.

This is like a bait-and-switch, where companies compare their product to a competitor's without disclosing that both options are environmentally harmful. **Example:** A company could claim its product is "more sustainable" than a competitor's, but both products still contribute to significant environmental damage.

As consumers, it's essential to look beyond greenwashing claims and demand transparency and accountability from the fashion industry. By avoiding these six sins of greenwashing and choosing brands with a true commitment to sustainability, we can positively impact the environment and support a more responsible and ethical fashion industry.

Talking about greenwashing is to become aware of this practice in order to distinguish between the real and the fake because, yes, obviously, there are plenty (and more and more) of truly sustainable, ethical, and responsible brands!

This book love to help so here are a few ways consumers can identify greenwashing and make informed decisions when shopping for ethical and sustainable products:

- **Check for third-party certifications:** Some third-party provide certifications for sustainable and ethical products. Checking for these certifications can help consumers determine whether a product is truly sustainable and ethical.
- **Look for transparency:** Brands that are truly sustainable and ethical should be transparent about their practices and supply chains. Look for brands that provide information about their materials, suppliers, and production processes (especially on their website, you know the 'about' page that people usually don't read).
- **Ask questions:** If a brand claims to be sustainable or ethical, but you're not sure, don't hesitate to ask questions. Brands that are truly sustainable and ethical should be willing to answer your questions and provide information about their practices.
- **Consider the whole picture:** When evaluating a brand's sustainability and ethics, it's important to

consider the whole picture, not just one aspect. For example, a brand that uses sustainable materials may not necessarily have fair labor practices.

By following these steps, you can make informed decisions when shopping for ethical and sustainable products, and help to reduce the impact of greenwashing in the market.

Here is an example of greenwashing ad:

Certified Sustainable T-shirt
Handmade with Vegan, natural and recycled material!

SAVE OUR PLANET

This ad is an example of greenwashing because it uses misleading claims and information to create the impression that the T-shirt is sustainable and environmentally friendly, when in fact, there is no evidence to support this claim.

Firstly, the **"Certified Sustainable T-shirt"** title is misleading because there is no proof of any certification. The brand is making an unsupported claim to attract environmentally conscious consumers.

Secondly, the description of the T-shirt being handmade with vegan, natural, and recycled materials is also misleading. The use of the terms **"handmade"** and **"vegan"** doesn't necessarily imply that the T-shirt was produced sustainably or that the workers were paid fairly. The use of **"natural"** materials doesn't necessarily mean that they are organic, pesticide-free, or even renewable. The use of **"recycled"** materials is also vague, as it doesn't indicate the percentage of recycled materials used or the source of those materials. It could be just the T-shirt label made with recycled materials.

Lastly, the message on the T-shirt, **"Save our planet,"** is misleading because there is no information about the production process or the environmental impact of making the T-shirt. It creates the impression that the T-shirt is sustainable and environmentally friendly, while in reality, there is no evidence to support this claim.

This ad is an example of greenwashing because it uses misleading claims and information to create the impression that the T-shirt is sustainable and environmentally friendly, when there is no evidence to support this claim.

Retro vs vintage, what's the difference?

Often confused, "retro" and "vintage" both refer to a notion of "old" yet have a distinct meaning, a meaning that makes all the difference when we are in the process of ethical fashion, aiming to limit our impact of overconsumption.

Retro: it is new clothes or objects but created according to an old look and inspiration. Retro clothing is, therefore, nothing more or less than a question of style. New clothes that imitate or are inspired by an older fashion, but therefore potentially from fast fashion or, in any case, from a new production of clothing.

Vintage: it's about authentic old clothes, well preserved and in good enough condition to be worn nowadays. Vintage clothes are, therefore, clothes with an old look because they are truly old and not recreated, nor are they the result of current fast fashion.

There you go! Now there's no excuse to confuse "retro" and "vintage"!

So, if you want to complete your wardrobe with pieces with an old look while remaining in an ethical fashion approach, go for vintage without hesitation! In addition to offering you clothes with a story, you will please yourself while respecting the planet, without participating or encouraging overproduction!

What does "Transparent" mean in fashion?

In fashion, "to be transparent" does not mean to have a translucent dress (ba-dun-tssh!).

In fact, in fashion, "to be transparent" or "being a transparent brand" means that all the manufacturing processes of a product are completely revealed and explained to the consumer.

From the origin or cultivation of the raw material to the transformation systems, to the workers and their working conditions, to the final rendering of the product, to the packaging and advertising techniques, to the shipping... all the stages of manufacturing are shown and explained to the consumers.

A transparent brand is not necessarily 100% responsible or organic or vegan or ethical (because nowadays it's still extremely complicated to be completely responsible)... but a transparent brand is **100% honest** towards its consumers, and as a consumer, it's still more pleasant to know and to be aware of what we buy!

You may wonder: Why aren't all brands transparent after all? Shouldn't we, as consumers, have the obvious right to know the origin and production methods of the products we purchase? What secrets do brands lacking in transparency keep from the public? What are they hiding, and/or what are they ashamed of?

Here is an example of a question we could all wonder as well:

Regardless of being very complicated for a brand to be 100% ethical and sustainable, they should at least be able to let you know where all the materials are coming from.

Have you ever wonder why some brands don't even precise what type of fabric is it that you find in their products, or where does it come from?

Maybe because, as we will reveal in the next questions of this book, it is almost impossible to completely trace back the origins of some fabrics, so, at the end, they can't be transparent about it because they don't even know, so would you actually trust someone who doesn't even know the answer while at the same time they are telling you how transparent they are?

TEXTILE
and its environmental impact

Natural or Organic clothing, what's the difference?

A natural product comes from nature (**#BreakingNews**)but is not subject to any rules or controlled by any organization, unlike an organic product.

A natural product can be cultivated with chemical products or fertilizers, even if they are bad for the workers or the environment, having received additional growth hormones or antibiotics... on the contrary to an organic product.

An organic product is usually grown or produced according to regulated standards that respect the environment and the well-being of workers.

For example, **cotton** fabric is a natural product that has been grown with many chemical fertilizers and pesticides and then treated with tons of synthetic products.

On the contrary, **organic cotton** fabric is a natural product grown in an ecological, responsible, and sustainable way, without chemicals or pesticides.

Another example would be leather, often promoted as a natural product, but is it really?

The raw material – the skin of an animal – is clearly natural, but once ripped off from an animal and treated with chemicals, it can no longer be considered "natural" because **it has been modified from its nature.**

These two examples are the greatest examples used by greenwashing; **just because it was born in nature does not always mean that it stays natural** once turned into a material, especially when their processes include pesticides, chemicals, dyes, bleach, etc., etc., etc.

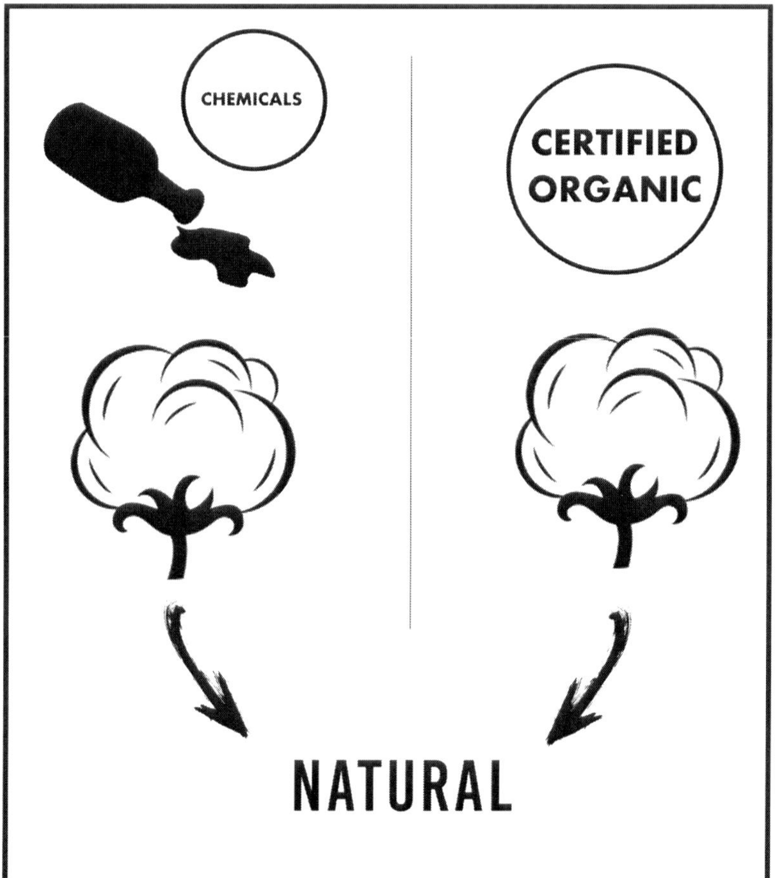
CHEMICALS
CERTIFIED ORGANIC
NATURAL

Cotton or organic cotton, what's the difference?

For a few years, we can see appearing in our stores, clothes, or fabrics in organic cotton. Greenwashing or real ecological benefit? What is really behind the name "organic cotton"... what is really behind cotton?

White, light, and from a natural fiber, it's hard to have a bad conscience when buying this fabric that has been dressing us for centuries, since birth, all over the world.

However, nowadays, in fast fashion, the production process of cotton requires the use of many synthetic agrochemicals that are extremely polluting, causing severe harm to the earth's air, water, soil, animals, and human health.

The International Cotton Advisory Committee (ICAC) states that though cotton occupies only **2.4% of global croplands**, it consumes **4.71% of global pesticides and 10.24% of all insecticides**[1]. These include insecticides and chemical fertilizers that cause disastrous effects on the soil, the environment, and the lives of farmers, or pesticides that pose a great threat to the world's freshwater resources and the animals living in these water.

Organic cotton is produced in an ecological, responsible, and sustainable way.

In fact, totally organically grown cotton plants are not genetically modified and do not require the use of toxic chemicals, harmful pesticides, or synthetic fertilizers. It also means that less water is being used in the process of creating the fabric, as well as no pigments or bleach, compared to conventional cotton, which by nature is not white. The natural color of cotton is slightly off-white, and while you can easily find this natural color in organic cotton fabric, conventional cotton needs to be dyed and bleached to get the bright white color we all used to think when we think of cotton.

In addition, organic cotton is often hand-picked, so workers are not affected by potentially toxic chemicals or any nuisance associated with machine harvesting.

According to the International Cotton Advisory Committee (ICAC), it takes an average of 1,931 liters of irrigation water and 6,003 liters of rainwater to produce 1kg of cotton lint[1]. That's equivalent to a T-shirt and a pair of jeans. If you're wondering how much water that really is, it's like taking **122 showers, filling up 70 bathtubs, or six years of drinking water**.

However, these figures represent a global average, and water consumption can vary significantly across regions. For instance, cotton farmers in the southeastern United States use an average of 234 liters of irrigated water per kilogram of cotton, whereas those in the western region use 3,272 liters. Therefore, it's crucial to consider the local and regional context when analyzing cotton production's water usage.

In Mekonnen and Hoekstra's 2011 global study[2], 33% of cotton's water use was attributed to the blue water footprint, 54% to the green water footprint, and 13% to the grey water footprint.

Textile Exchange conducted a study in 2014 comparing organic and conventional cotton and found that **organic cotton requires 91% less irrigation**[3].

In order to understand why organic cotton uses less water, it is important to understand the difference between blue, green, and grey water:

- **Blue water** refers to water that is directly consumed or withdrawn for agricultural, industrial, or domestic purposes. For example, when you turn on the tap to water your garden or take a shower, you're using blue water.

- **Green water,** on the other hand, is the total rainfall or soil moisture used to grow plants. This means that it's the water that is naturally available in the soil and from rainfall that is used by plants for growth. So, when you're growing a garden, the green water is what helps your plants thrive.

- **Grey water** refers to the volume of water needed to dilute and assimilate the pollutants present in wastewater to make it safe for the environment. This means that when you use water for activities like washing dishes, doing laundry, or taking a shower, the water becomes grey water because it has been contaminated with pollutants. This grey water needs to be treated before it can be safely released back into the environment.

Organic cotton production requires less water due to the health of the soil. Organic growing systems maintain a higher soil quality that reduces run-off into local rivers (grey water). Healthy soil can absorb and retain water for longer periods (green water), including droughts, resulting in less need for watering (blue water).

Textile Exchange state in their "Life Cycle Assessment (LCA) of Organic Cotton" report that 95% of the water used in organic cotton growing is green water[3].

Far from being a marketing term, organic certified cotton is truly respectful of the environment and all living communities. It is even particularly good for birds, fish, and other living creatures that depend on wetlands and rivers.

Just when you thought you had cotton all figured out, here's something new: cotton seeds are used to feed livestock, including dairy cattle and beef, and can also be crushed to produce oil for products such as salad dressing, cooking oil, and frying fats. Unfortunately, most of these seeds are genetically modified or chemically treated, which can have negative impacts on our food production systems. So, it turns out that your cotton purchases may actually impact your food choices too. **Who knew fashion could be so connected to food?**

We have, however, some bad and good news from OTA (Organic Trade Association)[4]:

The "bad" news is that only 0.95% of the global cotton production is organic cotton. Not so much, indeed, compared to conventional cotton.

The "Good" News is that in 2019/20, organic cotton fiber harvest increased by 31% compared to the previous harvesting year (2018/19), making it the second-largest organic cotton harvest record.

Consumers play an important role in driving the demand for organic cotton, and the more they choose organic cotton products, the more the textile industry is likely to become more sustainable. However, organic cotton is often more expensive than conventional cotton due to the cost of certification and the more sustainable farming practices used in its production. Nevertheless, the benefits to farmers, the environment, and human health make it a worthwhile investment.

FACT

Over 33% of global cotton farmers are based in India, where more than half (54%) of the annual pesticide usage is attributed to cotton cultivation[5].

Is bamboo fabric ecological?
Rayon, Viscose, Lyocell, Tencell, and Linen... What's the difference?

Bamboo has been a hot topic in the sustainability world, with its rapid growth and low need for pesticides, softer touch than cotton and promise of a "green" product by the big brands.

INBAR, the International Bamboo and Rattan Organization[1], reports that a Moso bamboo plantation that is well-managed can sequester roughly **32% more carbon dioxide** than an area of Chinese fir trees of equal size. In Colombia, research shows that Guadua, a type of tropical clumping bamboo, can trap about 60 tons per acre, approximately **58% more oxygen than trees, and absorbs up to 5 times more carbon**.

Indeed, we can easily understand the craze! But when it comes to clothing crafted from bamboo, the waters get murky.

There are different types of bamboo fabrics:

Rayon (also known as Viscose), the most commonly found "bamboo" fabric, is actually a manufactured fiber that is often made using environmentally harmful chemicals.

The typical process of making bamboo rayon, unless stated otherwise, is similar to that of conventional rayon (typically made of wood from eucalyptus, spruce, and pine trees). This process starts with the cellulose pulp of trees, a renewable resource, but requires harsh chemicals in the fiber-spinning phase. The commonly used method involves melting cellulose into xanthate, dissolving it in caustic soda, and regenerating cellulose through a spinneret. This process harms the environment, leaving a trail of waste as the water utilized can't be reused and gets often dumped into the groundwater along with contaminants. Employees in manufacturing facilities may also come into contact with these chemicals, leading to adverse health effects.

Regrettably, this is the most prevalent form of bamboo fabric on the market.

The Lyocell process is known for creating a more sustainable type of bamboo rayon called **Tencel**. This fabric production process operates in a closed loop cycle, which means that the chemicals and water used are continuously recycled and never released into the environment.

While Tencel, made from eucalyptus trees, is slightly less environmentally friendly than natural bamboo, it is a more affordable and commonly available option in the sustainable fashion industry.

Bamboo Linen. In this method, bamboo is shredded and then converted into a pulp through the use of natural enzymes. The natural fibers are then extracted and spun into yarn, similar to the process of making hemp or linen textiles (usually made from flax plant). This type of fabric also has a higher dye absorption rate, reducing the impact of the dyeing process in the supply chain. However, the downside is that the mechanical process is more costly and less available on an industrial scale compared to other textile manufacturing methods.

But how do you know you're getting the real thing and not just a rayon imposter?

The Federal Trade Commission has your back, stating that unless a product is made directly with bamboo fiber, it can't be called bamboo. For a product to be labeled and marketed as bamboo, the seller must provide scientific proof that it's made entirely of bamboo fiber[2].

It becomes more complex when considering that bamboo is typically grown without pesticides and doesn't require harmful chemicals to grow. This means that you can find on the market some rayon bamboo labeled as "organic." Even though bamboo is usually grown organically, making rayon involves many chemicals. So, if you spot any "organic" labels on bamboo rayon products, grab that greenwashing alarm and run the other way! Your wallet will thank you for finding a more truthful, sustainable option.

Beware! A lot of bamboo comes from areas with weak regulations, leading to the use of harmful chemicals and loss of habitats (including Giant Pandas' homes). Opt for **certified organic bamboo** to ensure it's grown responsibly and sustainably.

Is hemp the solution of tomorrow?

In recent years, we can see in stores and on the Internet more and more products derived from hemp.

Among these derivatives, textiles can also be found, which have quickly piqued the interest of ethical brands and designers in their quest for sustainable raw materials... Because, yes, hemp has many advantages and has quickly risen to the top of the list of ecological alternatives to cotton!

Hemp fabric is a **durable** textile made from fibers that come directly from the stalks of the Cannabis sativa plant.

Why is it great?

Already because the cultivation of hemp requires much **less water and land** area than cotton, producing up to twice the fiber yield per hectare[1,2].

Then because this environmentally friendly plant grows easily, without using agrochemicals, it can capture large amounts of carbon present in the environment, and it returns a large number of nutrients to the soil! (However, make sure to always choose organic to avoid any harmful chemicals in your clothes).

Experiences and scientific evidences have shown that hemp fabric is antibacterial and hypoallergenic by nature.[3]

And finally, when made into fabric, hemp is quite similar to the texture of cotton but stronger! It is very soft, light, breathable, and resistant to shrinking and pilling.

Hemp fabric is produced by extracting the long strands of fiber from the plant's stalk and separating them from the bark through a process called "retting." These fibers are then spun together to create a continuous thread, which can be woven into a fabric.

While the processing methods for hemp have been around since the early 1900s, they are now being updated to meet increasing demand.

Traditionally, the various stages of the hemp production process are carried out through a mechanical method that does not involve any harmful chemicals. However, some companies now opt for chemical production methods, which are more environmentally intensive but also faster and cheaper.

If a hemp fabric has been chemically treated, it is often labeled as "hemp viscose," which involves a similar harmful process as regular viscose, with the use of toxic chemicals. It is important to note that some companies use the less impactful lyocell process, so it is essential to double-check before purchasing any hemp products.

Is linen the solution of tomorrow?

If you're looking for a sustainable and stylish fabric that can make you feel like a Mediterranean yacht owner, look no further than linen. This incredible fabric is made from flax plant fibers and is not only one of the strongest and most durable materials in fashion history, but it's also one of the most biodegradable.

Linen's natural colors include ivory, ecru, tan, and grey, making it the perfect fabric for those who love a neutral, earthy color palette. It's also naturally moth resistant, so you can be sure your favorite linen pieces will last for years to come.

One of the most impressive things about linen is its ability to withstand high temperatures. It absorbs moisture without holding bacteria, which means it won't start to smell even in hot, humid environments.

And the best part? Linen actually gets better with age. It becomes softer and more pliable the more it is washed, and it's even stronger when wet than when dry. So not only will your linen pieces last a long time, but they'll also get better and better as time goes on.

But the benefits of linen don't stop there. Flax, the source material for producing linen, is a highly versatile plant. Linseed oil, a common by-product of flax, is great for wood preservation, and flaxseed oil is rich in omega 3. Plus, flax is a resilient plant that can thrive in poor soil, requiring significantly less water than cotton to grow.

According to the European Confederation of Linen and Hemp, only "4.52 L of water is necessary to produce 1kg of long scutched European Flax fibre"[1].

So, not only is linen a stylish and durable fabric, but it's also more sustainable than many other materials.

Of course, like any product, there are some downsides to linen. Non-organic linen may be treated with harmful dyes, and most non-organic flax is grown using nitrates, which can harm ecosystems if not used responsibly. That's why it's important to look for organic certifications or for brands that trace their linen products all the way back to the crop.

In the end, linen is the perfect fabric for those who want to look stylish and sustainable at the same time. It's strong, durable, biodegradable, and versatile.

So, the next time you're shopping for new clothes or home decor, be sure to give linen a second look. You won't be disappointed!

PU fabric or PVC, what's the difference?

When we talk about synthetic leather, there are two main types: **PU (Polyurethane) and PVC (Polyvinyl Chloride)**.

Both of them are used to make things like clothes, bags, and furniture, but they are different from each other in a few ways. Although PU (polyurethane) and PVC (polyvinyl chloride) come from the same source, fossil fuels, the manufacturing processes are not quite the same.

PU fabric is made by putting a special coating, called polyurethane, on a fabric like polyester. It's really good at looking and feeling like real leather. It's also lighter and can bend more easily. People like PU because it doesn't harm animals and is a bit better (less harmful) for the planet than PVC.

But PU isn't perfect. It can get damaged more easily than PVC and can deteriorate in high temperatures.

PVC, on the other hand, is made by adding plasticizers and dye to PVC, making it more flexible and suitable for coating onto a base fabric. It has been widely used in fashion due to its resemblance to leather and its waterproof properties (which is why it's great for raincoats and shoes), and is usually cheaper than PU.

However, PVC has some downsides too. It's not breathable, so it can be uncomfortable to wear. Also, making PVC can be worse for the environment because it releases harmful toxins into the air.

Speaking of the environment, that's one big difference between PU and PVC. PVC is known for being not so great for the planet, but PU isn't completely eco-friendly either.

They both come from sources that aren't renewable and need chemicals to be made.

In the end, whether you choose PU or PVC depends on your needs. If you want something that feels softer, is a bit kinder to the planet, and doesn't need to be super tough, PU is a better choice.

But if you're looking for something that's really strong, can keep water out, and doesn't cost too much, then PVC might be the one.

But let's face it; PU, PVC, Leather... Why not look at more natural and organic fabric? Maybe changing your perspective on fashion and looking for healthier alternatives will be more in line with who you are?

Because, remember: **Fashion is an external expression of yourself.**

Fabrics: Which one has the worst environmental impact?

A 2017 study titled "The pulse of the Fashion industry" by Global Fashion Agenda[1] ranks the fabrics and materials used by the fashion industry from the most harmful to the environment, workers, and animal welfare to the most respectful.

And if you also think that plastic products and synthetic textile fibers are at the top of this classification... continue to read, the top 3 may surprise you...

In fact, cowhide comes as number one, whose production processes are much worse than those of plastic. In second and third places, we still have no plastic nor synthetic fibers, but "natural" fibers since it is silk in second position and conventional cotton in third position. Number 4 you asked. Well still no Plastic, but wool.

We told you that you would be surprised

What can we do? Acknowledging that today in the fashion industry, the transformation and manufacturing processes are so bad, toxic, dangerous that even a natural raw material becomes chemical and worse than plastic...

You can take a little break recommended here to realize this truth that the industries are carefully trying to hide.

The good news is that there are some very clean (or less bad) alternatives to these catastrophic materials.

For example, choosing organic cotton over conventional cotton means choosing a fabric that requires less water consumption during production, less greenhouse gas emissions, and no use of insecticides or chemical fertilizers.

There are numerous materials available as substitutes for

leather that are significantly less harmful to the environment and the animals.

And even though, these alternatives might not be perfect since they still use a small percentage of plastic, many vegan alternatives are trying to reduce their use of it to have less impact on the environment (such as apple leather, grape leather, cactus leather, etc.).

Let's not forget that these alternatives are still new on the market but by being more conscious about the planet, they are trying to be on the right path to become completely plastic free.

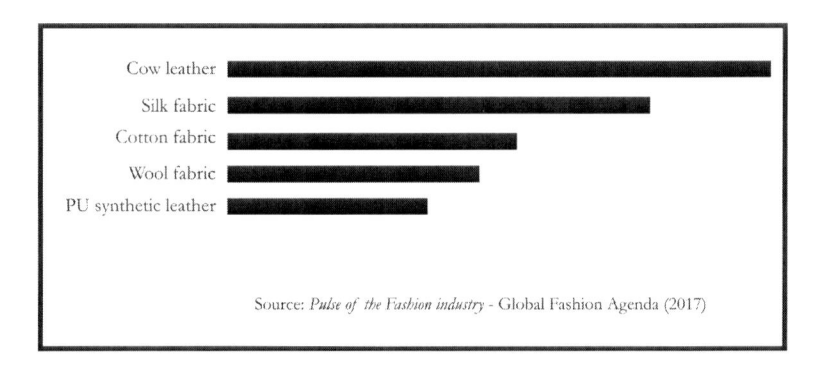

Cow leather	████████████████████████
Silk fabric	██████████████████
Cotton fabric	██████████
Wool fabric	████████
PU synthetic leather	█████

Source: *Pulse of the Fashion industry* - Global Fashion Agenda (2017)

ANIMALS

in fashion

Is leather a by-product of the meat industry?

No.
Not really.

A by-product is a secondary or incidental product that derives from a production process. Leather is often considered to be a by-product, meaning being the "waste" or "leftovers" of the meat industry and creating the idea of "upcycling" these remaining parts of the already dead animal instead of throwing it away.

#Greenwashing

In reality, leather is far from just an incidental result of meat production. Many animals are dedicated solely to leather production, proving that it is not just a by-product but a co-product.

So, what exactly is the difference between a by-product and a co-product?

A by-product is a secondary product that results from a production process, while a co-product is a product that is produced in addition to the main product and is often just as valuable as the main product.

For example, when cotton is harvested, we are left with cotton seeds, considered a by-product. However, if we modify the seeds through any process, such as crushing them to extract cottonseed oil, the oil becomes a co-product.

Similarly, rawhide may be considered a by-product (that will probably rot in a couple of days). But, after undergoing the processes of tanning and dying, it becomes a co-product... Or a brand-new product in its own right.

So, next time someone tries to tell you that leather is just a waste product, you can proudly educate them on the truth. Leather is a co-product —No more "leftover" talk!

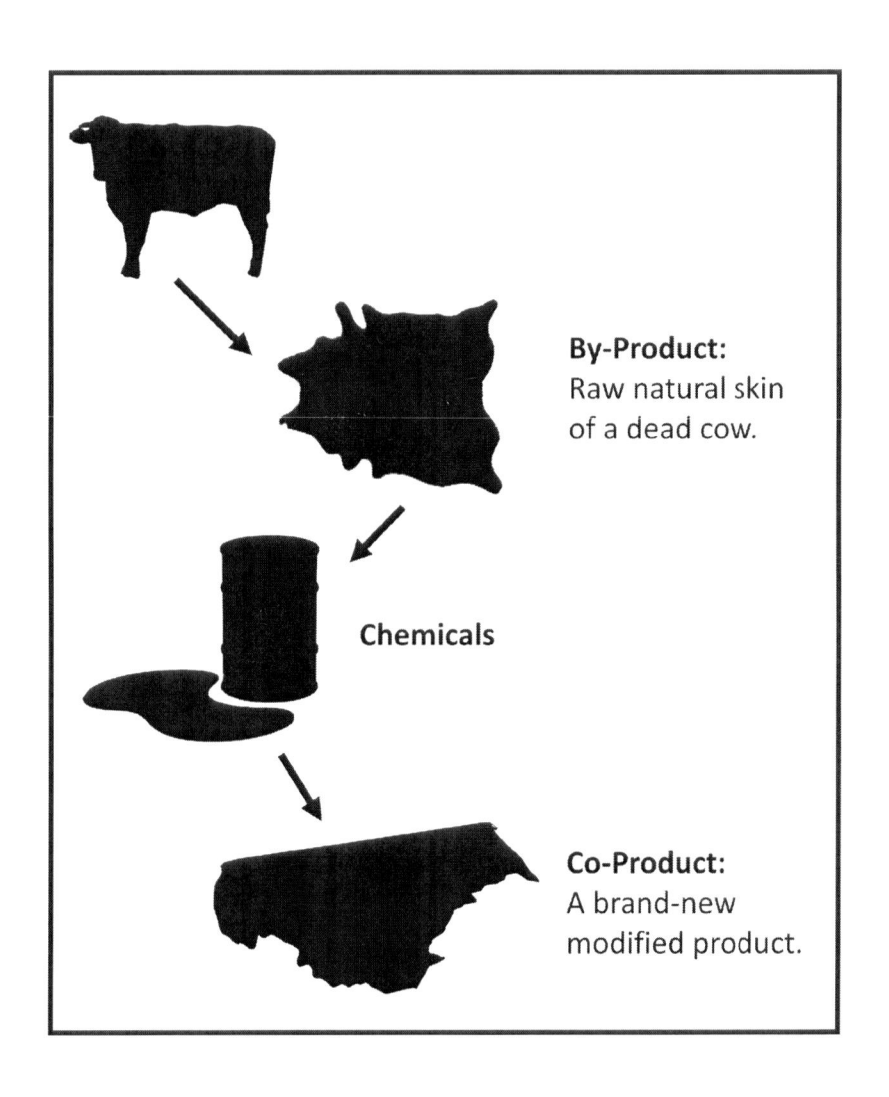

By-Product: Raw natural skin of a dead cow.

Chemicals

Co-Product: A brand-new modified product.

Chemicals - Which ones are used to create leather?

Leather comes from the skin of animals. **#BreakingNews**

Or to be more precise, leather is (literally) the skin of animals. But transformed. And when you think about it... It seems quite logical, otherwise it would be impossible to wear as a jacket or a shoe; Nobody want a rotten smelly hide on the shoulders.

The number one problem with leather (beyond the fact that an animal must be killed) is that in order to transform this raw material, the leather has to be treated with tons of extremely toxic and environmentally dangerous chemicals.

Among these chemicals, we find the worst of all: **chromium 6**.

But also, mineral salts, formaldehyde, coal tar derivatives, various oils, dyes, and finishes (some of which are cyanide-based), etc...

Chrome tanning accounts for over 90% of the world's leather production[1], and depending on the tannery **between 50 and 250 chemicals are used per leather piece**[2]. These chemicals are used to burn the hair, bleach the hide, make the leather shine, dye, preserve or soften it more quickly, making the transformation process go from what normally would be at least two months to only 24 hours, from raw material (an animal) to usable material (the future bag).

Sean Gallagher's documentary *"The Toxic Price of Leather"*[2] highlights that Kanpur became India's top exporter of leather products in 2013, with 95% of the city's leather goods being sent to countries such as the United States, the United Kingdom, Germany, Italy, and China.

However, the tanneries in Kanpur generate **50 million liters of highly toxic wastewater each day**, of which only 20% is properly treated before being released onto local farmland or into the River Ganges. This untreated wastewater is laced with dangerous levels of chromium, lead, and arsenic. Consequently, local residents suffer from a range of health issues, including mental disabilities, tuberculosis, eyesight problems, skin discoloration, and asthma, among others. The documentary also shows children playing in this contaminated water, exposing them to these hazardous toxins.

Due to the high toxicity of leather production, a significant majority (95%) of **tanneries in the United States have relocated their operations overseas** to evade penalties related to environmental oversight[3].

While the skin retains some of the chemicals used, most are released into wastewater, severely polluting the workspace, waterways, public settlements, and the environment more generally.

A French documentary titled "CUIR, les forçats de la mode"[4] reveals that some tanneries in India continue to use mercury, a chemical that has been banned in Europe for over 20 years. It also shows that the leftover leather is combined with an acid and sold as feed for fish and chickens. **Buying cheap leather can have an impact on the food system.**

The documentary also exposes the **daily use of child labor in these tanneries**, where children **under 12 years old work every single day** without proper equipment or protective gear for 21€ per month. Despite the existence of laws, these practices continue to persist.

The second problem with leather (and one that puts us in a bit of a bind) is that it is almost impossible to clearly trace all the leather transformation processes, or to clearly define how many or which chemicals were actually used (especially since each factory uses a different technique/recipe).

So, to conclude, this question can't be answered completely and accurately... That is a bit embarrassing... or should the fashion industry be the one feeling embarrassed instead?

To go even further, you will find below a summary table from ISTT (International School of Tanning Technology)[4] of the most commonly used chemicals for the tanning process of leather.

Keep in mind that this is supposed to be one of the best practices when using chemicals (this list is not exhaustive, because really, we can't trace everything clearly):

Beamhouse and Tanyard:

- **Biocides** inhibit the development of bacteria that can harm the hides or skins during the soaking process.
- **Surfactants** are used to help with the wetting back of the hides or skins.
- **Degreasers** help with the removal of natural fats and greases from the hides or skins.
- **Swell regulating agents** help prevent uneven swelling of the hides or skins during liming
- **Lime** is used to swell the hides or skins.
- **Sodium sulphide** chemically destroys the hair on hides or skin.
- **Sodium hydrosulphide** chemically destroys the hair on hides or skins. It does not create as much swelling as sodium sulphide.
- **Low sulphide unhairing agents** help to reduce the

amount of sulphides used in a tannery thus reducing the environmental impact of tanneries.
- **Caustic soda** is used during the liming process to help swell the hides or skins.
- **Soda ash** is used during the soaking or liming processes to help raise the pH of the hides or skins.
- **Liming auxiliaries** reduce the wrinkling or uneven swelling of the hide during the liming process by helping with the even penetration of the liming chemicals into the hide.
- **Ammonium sulphate** is used during the deliming process and helps remove lime from the hides or skins.
- **Ammonium chloride** is used during the deliming process and helps remove lime from the hides or skins.
- **Organic - acid deliming chemicals** are used to replace traditional ammonium salts when deliming hides and skins. They thus help reduce the ammonium salt pollution in tannery wastewaters.
- **Sodium metabisulphite** is used during the deliming process and helps prevent the formation of toxic hydrogen sulphide gas during deliming. It also acts as a bleaching agent.
- **Formic acid** is used during the pickling process to lower the pH of the hides or skins. It acts as a buffer and helps prevent a very low pH during the pickling process.
- **Sulphuric acid** is used during the pickling process to lower the pH of the hides or skins. It is a very strong acid and results in a very low pH during the pickling process is used on its own.

- **Salt** is used during the pickling process to prevent acid swelling of the hides or skins.
- **Salt-free pickling chemicals** are used to replace the traditional use of salt in the pickling process. They have a significant impact on reducing the salts present in tannery wastewaters.
- **Sodium formate** is used during the tanning process to assist with the penetration of chromium tanning salts into the hides or skins.
- **Chromium sulphate** is the tanning agent used to make wet blue.
- **Aldehydes** are tanning agents used to make wet white.
- **Magnesium oxide** is used during basification and raises the pH of the hide or skin to allow the chromium or aldehyde to chemically bind to the skin protein.
- **Sodium bicarbonate** can also be used during the basification process to raise the pH of the hide or skin to allow the chromium or aldehyde to chemically bind to the skin protein.
- **Fungicides** are chemicals that are used to prevent the growth of moulds or fungi on tanned hides or skins

Dyehouse:

- **Surfactants** help in the wetting back of the wet blue or wet white in the dyehouse. They reduce the wetting back time and also help clean the wet blue or wet white, removing dirt or machine grease or oil.
- **Degreasers** help remove grease or fats that may be

present on the wet blue or wet white as a result of the wet blue or wet white coming into contact with tanning machinery.
- **Sodium formate** helps raise the pH during the neutralization process.
- **Sodium bicarbonate** helps raise the pH during the neutralization process.
- **Neutralizing syntans** help raise the pH during the neutralization process.
- **Formic acid** reduces the pH for the rechroming process or helps with chemically fixing dyehouse chemicals to the leather at the end of the dyehouse processes.
- **Chrome syntans** are used during rechroming to improve the softness of the final leather and improve the dye levelness.
- **Chromium sulphate** is used during rechroming to improve the softness of the final leather and improve the dye levelness.
- **Syntans** are used to give properties such as softness, fullness, roundness to the leather.
- **Resins** are used to give fullness, good lightfastness and a tight grain to the leather.
- **Polymers** are used to give fullness, good lightfastness and a tight grain to the leather.
- **Dyes** are used to give the leather a colour desired by the customer.
- **Dyeing auxiliaries** help disperse the dyes evenly giving better dye penetration and a more level colour.
- **Fatliquors** are oils that are added to leather to give softness to the final leather

Finishing

- **Acrylic resins** give specific properties to the leather finish such as adhesion, water resistance.
- **Butadiene resins** give specific properties to the leather finish such as good coverage.
- **Polyurethane resins** give specific properties to the leather finish such as good toughness and good lightfastness.
- **Fillers** help fill small blemishes on the leather surface and prevent the leather sticking to the embossing plate or roller when it is embossed.
- **Dullers** help reduce the gloss of the finish.
- **Crosslinkers** are used to toughen the leather finish and improve the water resistance properties of polyurethanes.
- **Handle modifiers** are used to give the leather surface a waxy or slippery feel and help improve some of the test performance results.
- **Nitrocellulose lacquers** are used in the top coat of a leather finish.
- **Acrylic lacquers** are used in the top coat of a leather finish.
- **Polyurethane lacquers** are used in the top coat of a leather finish.
- **Viscosity modifiers** are used to increase the viscosity of a finish mixture.
- **Pigments** are colouring agents that help hide defects on the leather surface.
- **Dyes** are colouring agents that are used to slightly change the colour of the leather finish or to give the leather finish a more natural look.

- **Defoamers** are used to prevent bubbles from forming in the finish mixture

As you can see, even leather has some polyurethane (plastic) for its finishing part.

Do you still believe leather is a natural product?

"LEATHER IS A NATURAL PRODUCT" DEBUNKED

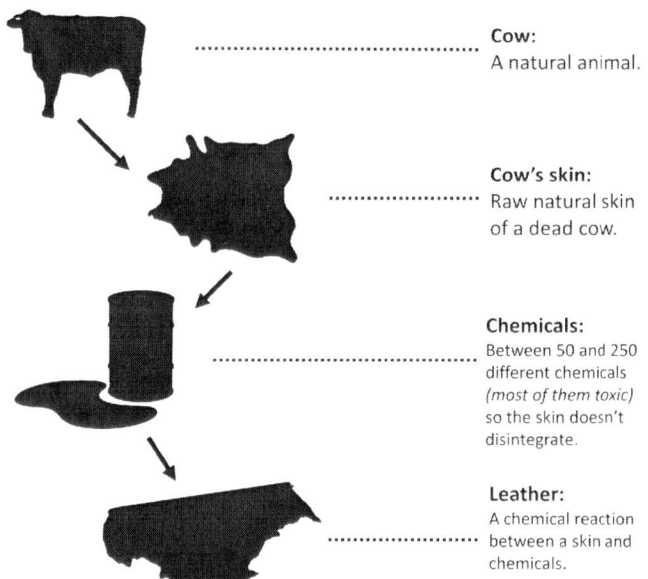

Cow:
A natural animal.

Cow's skin:
Raw natural skin of a dead cow.

Chemicals:
Between 50 and 250 different chemicals *(most of them toxic)* so the skin doesn't disintegrate.

Leather:
A chemical reaction between a skin and chemicals.

Conclusion: **Leather is as natural as plastic.**

What is Chromium?

Chromium 3 is an ultra-oligo-mineral mainly present in plant and animal tissues. It is called an "essential trace element" because a minimum amount of chromium is necessary for human health; in fact, some people take chromium supplements to improve their blood sugar levels or to prevent metabolic syndrome.

So far, it sounds like a good chemical our body needs, and if we were to stop explaining about it here, there would be nothing wrong with it...

However, when heated to high temperatures and processed, **chromium 3 becomes chromium 6** (also known as Chromium VI and Hexavalent chromium) , an extremely harmful and carcinogenic chemical, hazardous to human health and the environment.

Workers in the tanning industry who use chrome have reportedly suffered from a variety of health issues, including mental disabilities, tuberculosis, eyesight problems, skin discoloration, and asthma, among others.[1]

Unfortunately, **90% of the world's leather is tanned with harmful chemicals**[1] **including chromium 6, arsenic, and formaldehyde** that cause serious harm to workers. In addition, chromium is a major pollutant in waterways and the environment in general.

A documentary[2] revealed that many individuals in Europe had been exposed to chromium 6, having dangerous allergic reactions. It also featured a chemist working in the import industry who stated that over 99% of containers are not tested for toxicity. The testing process for detecting chromium 6 in leather requires a lengthy and costly laboratory test. In the documentary, 50 pairs of shoes were tested and it was discovered that over 40% of them contained significant amounts of chromium 6, exceeding the levels considered safe.

According to research conducted by Kazi Madina Maraz[3], chrome-tanned leather, even in its finished form, can be environmentally hazardous. For example, burning leather seats from scrapped cars can release toxic chromium VI into the atmosphere.

Many leather company owners will argue that chromium tanning was created in the 90s, so how they were producing leather before that? Well, before the introduction of chromium tanning, the demand of leather was not as high, and there was no need for fast and cheap production methods.

Today, only a few tanneries (less than 9%) use vegetable tanning leather and claim that it is a better solution, but is it really? Let's explore this in our next question!

Is vegetable tanning / veg-tan of animal leather an ethical and ecological solution?

Let's play a game!

Try to spot the greenwashing in this sentence:

"Vegetable-tanned leather is biodegradable, has a low impact on our environment, and is natural and very common."

Did you find it?

Yes, the entire sentence is pure greenwashing!

"Vegetable-tanned leather is biodegradable"

The tanning process aims to turn organic skin into inorganic leather (so it won't rot on your shoulders). This process's primary goal is to ensure that leather doesn't biodegrade. If we want the hide to be biodegradable, we shouldn't tan them in the first place.

"Vegetable-tanned leather has a low impact on our environment"

To have a skin of an animal, we need an animal (Duh!). This means that we need land, food, and water; as you probably already know, animals release a lot of methane. The process of vegetable tanning takes months and uses a lot of water.

A vegetable-tanned leather will always be better than chrome-based tanning leather, but **calling it sustainable or saying that it has a low impact on our environment is pure greenwashing.**

The study "Measuring the Environmental Footprint of

Leather Processing Technologies"[1] found that there are no notable differences in the environmental impact between the vegetable and chromium leather tanning processes. Although using renewable materials such as tree bark is a better option than using chromium, this study shows that overall environmental impact is still similar between the two methods.

"Vegetable-tanned leather is natural and very common"

Well, as soon as we modify a raw material, it becomes, by definition, unnatural. Saying that leather is natural is like saying that plastic is a natural chemical reaction between natural oil and natural alcohol. The chromium tanning process is way faster and four times cheaper; this is why 90% of the leather industry uses it, leaving tiny space for the vegetable version... So, no, vegetable-tanned leather isn't common.

But how is it done?

The tanning process is just one step in the transformation of skin into leather; just like chrome-tanned, vegetable-tanned leather needs to go through several chemicals.

Lime, or calcium oxide, is one of these chemicals, and it can cause skin irritation and burns if it comes into contact with the skin. Lime removes the hair, proteins, and some layers of the skin on the hide so that it can be tanned.

Vegetable tanning leather is made using natural materials, such as bark, leaves, and roots, to process and tan the animal hides. The process involves soaking the hides in a series of baths containing tannins, which are naturally occurring compounds found in plants. These tannins bind to the proteins in the hide, transforming it into leather.

Although the vegetable tanning process (40 to 60 days on average) takes longer than other tanning methods, such as chrome tanning (1 to 2 days), it results in a more natural-looking leather that is more durable and develops a unique patina over time. However, more time means more water and energy usage.

Many leather companies prefer chrome tanning because it is faster, cheaper, and results in a softer leather that is easier to dye.

FACT

Chrome tanning is not ready to stop since many leather manufacturers continue to use it as they believe it produces a more versatile and desirable material overall.

Pee in leather?

Urine, an unexpected but significant substance, held a pivotal role in ancient leatherworking.

Its importance was so pronounced that the ancient Romans established a thriving trade in collected urine from public urinals, even subjecting urine traders to taxation[1] by the Latin emperor Vespasian (Latin: vectigal urinae - Urine tax).

This raises the question: **What made pee so valuable to preindustrial societies?**

This "liquid gold" has always played a crucial part in scientific and industrial advancements. Its composition, particularly the presence of urea, made it an invaluable resource. Stored for extended periods, urine's urea would decompose into ammonia[2], a compound with unique properties that captivated the attention of preindustrial humans.

Leatherworkers of ancient times uncovered the capabilities of ammonia in the leather production. They soaked animal hides in containers filled with urine[3]. As time passed, the ammonia effectively penetrated the hide fibers, breaking down structural proteins and transforming the hides into pliable and workable leather.

The significance of urine in leatherworking didn't end there. It played an instrumental role in hair and flesh removal from the hides, streamlining the leather production process. The high pH and ammonia content of urine facilitated the dissolution and loosening of unwanted elements, leaving behind clean and pristine hides for the leather artisans.

While the idea of using urine in leather production may

seem strange and unappealing in the present day, it highlights the adaptability and innovative spirit of humanity. It challenges our perceptions about waste and value, reminding us that true ingenuity can arise from the most unexpected sources.

So, the next time you admire a historical crafted leather item, pause and reflect upon the ancient secret behind its creation – **the surprising role of pee in leather.**

Plastic in leather?

It may come as a surprise to many, but **plastic materials are commonly used in the production of traditional leather**.

One of the primary reasons for this is to enhance the leather's water resistance. To achieve this, leather manufacturers often apply a polyurethane (PU) coating or film to the surface of the leather. This coating creates a barrier that prevents water from penetrating the leather, making it more durable and long-lasting.

Furthermore, plastic materials are also used to give leather desirable properties such as a smooth texture or a glossy finish. For instance, some manufacturers use a PVC coating to produce a shiny leather look.

Despite the "benefits" that plastic materials provide in traditional leather production, there are environmental and ethical concerns associated with their use. Plastic production relies on fossil fuels, which emit greenhouse gases that contribute to climate change. Additionally, plastic waste can cause harm to the environment and wildlife by polluting landfills and waterways and disrupting ecosystems.

Therefore, the use of plastic materials in traditional leather production raises important questions about sustainability and responsible environmental practices.

A research conducted by the F.A.K.E. movement (Fashion for Animal Kingdom & Environment), in collaboration with VegFund, aimed to analyze various pieces of leather from fast fashion items and determine their origin[1] by using optical microscopy. However, the researchers were only able to identify the species of 40% of the leather tested. The remaining samples had their hair follicles removed, making the identification more difficult, possibly due to the use of harsh chemicals during the tanning process.

What was even more surprising was that the majority of the leather samples contained layers of polyurethane, textile (nylon), rubber, or foam to make it thicker. This shows that many companies are using various methods to produce leather more quickly and cost-effectively. The high demand for leather has driven manufacturers to find ways to cut corners.

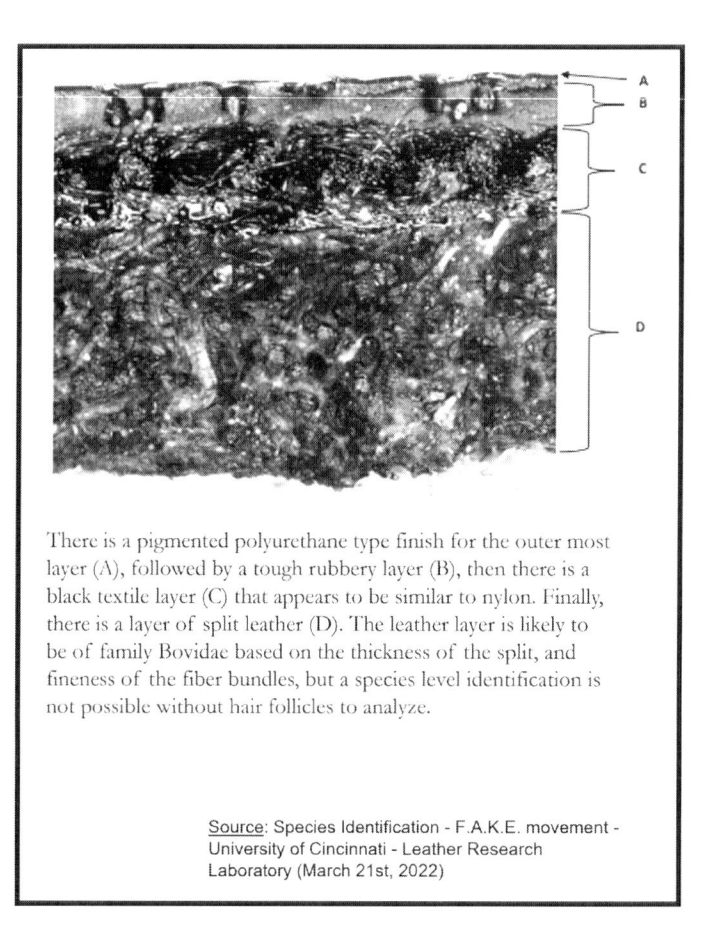

There is a pigmented polyurethane type finish for the outer most layer (A), followed by a tough rubbery layer (B), then there is a black textile layer (C) that appears to be similar to nylon. Finally, there is a layer of split leather (D). The leather layer is likely to be of family Bovidae based on the thickness of the split, and fineness of the fiber bundles, but a species level identification is not possible without hair follicles to analyze.

Source: Species Identification - F.A.K.E. movement - University of Cincinnati - Leather Research Laboratory (March 21st, 2022)

What is genuine leather?

First of all, let's take a look at the structure of the leather.

Leather has a few different layers. The top layer, or "grain," is the part you can see and feel, and it's what gives the leather its reputation. The middle layer, called the corium, is where the bulk of the fibers are, giving the leather its strength and structure. Finally, there's the flesh layer, which is the underside of the leather.

Now, let's talk about "genuine leather." This term is a bit of a misnomer because it's actually the lowest quality of all the leathers. What some companies do is take the middle layer, throw it in a blender with some glue, and press it into a sheet. If you're "lucky", they'll add a thin sheet of top grain, but usually, it's just coated with layers of PVC to give it a leather look and feel.

It's the cheapest of all the leathers, literally made from scraps of other kinds of leather. It is the weakest of all leathers.

Identifying the animal from which the leather originated becomes even more complicated due to this process.

But here's the real kicker: some companies are using the "genuine leather" label to sell products made from some truly questionable materials. Cats, dogs, pigs, and other animals have been found in products labeled as "genuine leather." These companies know that no one would buy products made from these animals if they were labeled as such, so they hide behind the "genuine leather" label to avoid scrutiny.

So, how can you protect yourself from these shady practices? Well... Maybe you shouldn't buy leather in the first place.

Cat and dog leather... Does it really exist?

Unfortunately, yes.

But that shouldn't shock us more than cowhide; at the end of the day, **an animal is an animal regardless of their species**.

The oldest evidence of humans eating dogs dates back to approximately 9,260 years ago[1]. This evidence was found in naturally preserved human feces at a rock shelter known as Hinds Cave in Texas, where a dog bone was discovered. This provides the earliest evidence of human consumption of dogs in the world.

In several countries, cows are not the only victims of the fashion industry. Cats and dogs are as well killed for their meat and skin. At least, they used to be.

An investigation made by PETA[2] has confirmed that China was shipping to the United States cat and dog's leather disguised as "real leather" or even as "lamb leather". This undercover investigation shows dogs being killed, hit, bashed over the head with a wooden pole, and skinned in front of other dogs.

Once their skin has been processed and transformed into fabric, it is impossible for a consumer to recognize what kind of cow breed the industry is using to make that shiny leather when in fact, they might as well be using cat and dog's leather.

An employee revealed to the investigator that approximately **100 to 200 dogs were beaten and skinned daily** in this facility. At the time of the video recording, around 300 dogs were present on the premises, awaiting their turn for slaughter.

The owner of the plant stated that he had approximately 30,000 partially processed pieces of dog leather in stock. This leather was used in various dog-leather accessories, including gloves, and is produced in factories like these and sold worldwide.

Once the leather has been labeled as "real leather" or "lambskin" coming from China, it is technically impossible to know what kind of leather it actually is without going through the process of laboratory studies and analyses.

To give you a perspective on the issue, a group of scientists conducted a study in 2015 to determine the species of leather by analyzing its DNA[3].

This study was sponsored by Hermes, who wanted to uncover any fraudulent practices (such as promoting chamois leather when it wasn't), and also by the French music museum "Musée de la musique", which sought to identify the leather found in an old piano.

Scientists had to reconstruct damaged DNA due to the tanning process in order to identify the species of leather, a complex and costly process. I had the chance to talk to the main researcher over a Zoom call, who explained to me that these studies can cost tens of thousands of dollars and only provide a guess of the species without 100% accuracy.

Meanwhile, the U.S. Customs and Border Protection warns that brands that import cat or dog skin may face a fine of up to $10,000[4], but this amount is not significant for big fast fashion brands. These brands often use subcontractors and can claim ignorance of the fact that the leather came from cats or dogs since the products are labeled as "genuine leather."

As mentioned in a previous question "Plastic in leather?",

we conducted research to identify the species of animals used in various leather samples[5]. However, the process was expensive and not successful in identifying the species. This means that even if one wanted to prove that a fashion brand uses dog or cat leather, it would require a significant investment of resources with a potentially limited impact on the brand.

So when you buy a product labeled as "genuine leather", or even "100% leather," brands can add whatever they want in the recipe of this leather: foam, rubber, textile, plastic, or even dog leather. Can you imagine buying bread, looking at the ingredients and only seeing: ingredients = bread.

In May 2020, China introduced the ban on selling live dogs and dog meat for food[6]. It was a memorable moment for animal welfare; it was the first time in history that dogs were recognized as companion animals, not food for humans.

Many countries still allow the consumption of dog meat. However, the absence of concrete evidence makes it challenging to determine the current status of dog leather production. One thing for sure is that all of the above proves that it is still possible, and dog leather (probably labeled as genuine leather) might still be on the market.

But, it begs the question, **what is the actual difference between cow leather and leather made from dogs or other animals?**

Kangaroo leather?

Kangaroo leather is a type of leather made from the tanned skin of kangaroos, native Australian marsupials. It is known for its softness, thinness, and flexibility, making it a favored material for sports shoes and gloves.

Labeling kangaroo leather as "k-leather" is a common practice that may mislead consumers into buying the product without complete awareness of its true source. Using such generic labels obscures the fact that "k-leather" refers to the skin of kangaroos, potentially disconnecting consumers from the ethical and environmental implications of their purchasing choices

This lack of transparency highlights the need for greater awareness and education regarding the true nature of kangaroo leather, allowing consumers to make informed decisions about the products they support.

But why Kangaroo leather (or K-leather) has such an ethical concern? These concerns stem from various factors associated with the industry's practices and their impact on animals and ecosystems.

One of the primary controversies surrounding kangaroo leather is the ethical treatment of kangaroos during hunting and harvesting processes. The documentary "Kangaroo: A love hate story" by Mick and Kate McIntyre[1] shows that Kangaroos are typically shot and killed at night in rural areas. These inhumane killings and unnecessary suffering raise significant animal welfare concerns.

Moreover, monitoring and enforcing ethical practices in kangaroo hunting and culling are challenging due to the remote locations where these activities take place. While codes of practice exist to guide the proper treatment of kangaroos, ensuring compliance remains an ongoing struggle.

Another issue associated with kangaroo leather is the lack of transparency in supply chains. Due to the complexity of sourcing and processing kangaroo hides, brands using kangaroo leather may find it challenging (or clearly impossible) to ensure ethical and sustainable practices throughout their supply chains. This opacity can result in unknowingly supporting unethical practices and failing to provide consumers with accurate information regarding the origins of their products.

Additionally, the chemicals and processes involved in the tanning and treatment of kangaroo hides can have environmental consequences. Pollution from wastewater and the use of toxic substances can harm local ecosystems and water sources.

It is crucial to consider as well the perspectives of Indigenous communities when discussing kangaroo leather. While some Indigenous cultures have traditionally used kangaroo skins for various purposes, it is important to recognize that Indigenous views on the commercial kangaroo industry are diverse. Some Indigenous voices highlight the inherent rights of kangaroos as native animals and express concerns about the commodification and exploitation of these species.

As outlined in the report "A Shot in the Dark" by a wildlife ecologist[2], a troubling yearly practice exposes an estimated **440,000 dependent young kangaroos** to either a savage outcome through battering or a tragic fate of starvation following the loss of their mothers' lives.

Exotic leather, how luxurious it is?

Exotic leather has long captivated the fashion industry, renowned for its luxurious texture and unique aesthetics. From crocodile and snake to ostrich and lizard, the allure of these exotic skins has attracted designers and consumers alike. However, the production and use of exotic leather raise significant ethical and environmental concerns.

The ethical implications of exotic leather are a primary source of contention. Obtaining exotic skins often involves the capturing, confinement, and killing of wild animals, disrupting their natural habitats and potentially endangering species' populations. The methods employed to obtain these skins can be inhumane and cruel, leading to unnecessary suffering and loss of biodiversity.

A recent investigation conducted by PETA[1] sheds light on the unethical practices involving one-year-old crocodiles in Zimbabwe and Texas. Disturbing footage reveals workers ruthlessly stabbing conscious alligators in an attempt to dislocate their vertebrae, despite a manager acknowledging that "reptiles will continue to live" even after such actions. The investigator observed alligators displaying signs of life, as they continued to move their legs and tails.

Another major concern surrounding exotic leather lies in the lack of transparency within its supply chains. The complex nature of sourcing exotic skins, often from countries with weak regulations, makes it challenging to trace the origins of the leather. This opacity makes it difficult for consumers to make informed choices and support ethically produced goods. **Without transparency, there is a higher risk of unknowingly contributing to unsustainable and**

unethical practices.

The production of exotic leather poses significant environmental challenges as well. The demand for exotic skins drives habitat destruction and wildlife exploitation. Deforestation, pollution from tanneries, and the use of toxic chemicals in the tanning process contribute to environmental degradation and ecosystem disruption. Additionally, raising exotic animals for their skins can require vast amounts of resources, including water and food, further straining ecosystems and exacerbating climate change.

Do you still believe exotic leather is a luxurious "product"?

Human leather... Really?

If you think cat and dog leather is creepy enough, wait for us to tell you all about human leather.

Yes, human leather... made out of humans, like you and me.

To begin with, a couple of years ago, a website called humanleather.com[1] was apparently producing and selling products made of human leather. According to them, they created this type of fabric, in a very ethical and legal way, from the skin of people who gave full consent to use their skin after their death.

But does their consent make this subject morally approved rather than plain creepy? Or does this create any kind of repulsion? Because if so, shouldn't the use of an animal's skin should be as repulsive, considering it is still a life taken apart?

To creep you more out, what would you say if we told you that a project had created the concept of growing human leather in laboratories with the DNA of a person?

Tina Gorjanc created this concept[2] for her final master's project with the idea to grow a human leather fabric from DNA and not just any; she patented the concept to use the DNA from the late designer Alexander McQueen.

Yes, you read it!

How about that now? **Would you be willing to wear a jacket made of your favorite designer's DNA? Or even of a late member of your family?**

Her work was purely conceptual as she only patented the idea, which was the actual point of the project: the concern of biological information protection.

Nobody told her it was illegal to collect hair from a dead person found in some of his old collections and transform it into the fabric, so if nobody stopped her, a student, then who would stop any big corporation that would want to execute this idea if there is no legal regulation?

In the end, she made her collection using pig's leather (to her point of view because "it's the closest to look like human skin")

Isn't this ironic and more likely very unfair to be concerned about it when it is what the whole animal industry is all about? The exploitation of animals just for our own pleasure! Where are the laws against it? And more importantly, who is fighting to get them? The animals can't because they can't speak. They, unfortunately, can't shout out in any human language, and just because they are not able to phonetically give out consent, then it's ok to take it?

In those two examples, human rights are an absolute necessity, but why should we ignore animal rights?

So, please ask yourself this very important question: **why do we think is creepy, wrong and it should be illegal to use the skin of a human, but it is completely normal to use the skin of an animal?** What is the difference? Culture? Habits? History? Religion? The food chain?

We as humans are the kings of the world? Yes, yes, we all heard all of that before, but take all those excuses away and what do we get? Nothing but the fact that animals should have rights of living as humans do.

Is wool ethical?

We know wool comes from sheep, more specifically from "sheep's hair." We also know that sheep's wool naturally becomes thicker during winter to protect themselves against the cold, and it has to be shed during spring to stop them from suffocating, so basically, we are actually helping out sheep to keep on living, while only "cutting" off their unnecessary hair… just like a haircut, so, painless right?

Well, yes, and no.

Yes, we do actually have to shed the wool of sheep to stop the suffocation.

No, we wouldn't be doing it if it wasn't for the fashion industry.

Naturally, sheep would grow only the necessary amount of wool that they need to keep warm, and they naturally shed some of their wool each year.

At least that was entirely true until humans started to breed sheep, such as Merinos, which after being selectively bred and genetically modified in order to produce more wool, the natural process of wool grown doesn't exist anymore, so we do must shed the sheep's wool for them not to suffer. However, it is not at all, just like a haircut.

Despite the efforts of PETA organizations worldwide to expose shocking **cruelty at 117 farms across six countries and four continents**[1], the wool industry has shown little to no signs of change or improvement.

Sheep are either sheared too early (before the wool begins to fall naturally and lose quality), which sometimes leads to the death of some of these animals due to the cold weather, or they are sheared too late (to let the wool grow to its full length), which sometimes leads to the death of some of these animals who suffocate under too much heat or too much weight.

Many investigations have shown that sheep are very badly mistreated at the time of shearing, often resulting in numerous cuts and injuries[1]. (It is difficult to do it right when you want to do it in a chain, always faster, with a living animal struggling between your arms).

Typically, shearers are compensated based on the number of sheep they shear rather than the time spent, incentivizing them to work quickly without prioritizing the welfare of the sheep. This approach often results in frequent injuries as the sheep are mishandled.

Numerous reports have surfaced highlighting instances of unnecessary beating and harm inflicted on sheep during the shearing process[1].

Sheep go through a cruel procedure called "**mulesing**" which is the removal of skin around a sheep's buttocks, made in order to prevent a parasite infection called "flystrike," a procedure that often leads to exposed, bloody wounds leading to worse infections and even death.

According to the National Wool Declaration (NWD)[2], the percentage of wool produced using mulesing practices increased to **74%** in July 2021, a significant jump from the 18% recorded in 2008.

Sheep also go through another cruel procedure called "**dipping**" a procedure that means that sheep are fully immersed in chemical[3], insecticide, or herbicide solutions to eliminate harmful parasites, which is not only awful to the sheep due to the fact that with the dipping, they are exposed to be intoxicated leading to several health problems, but it is also dangerous for the people[4] implementing the dipping because they can be poisoned by these chemicals and of course, completely environmentally catastrophic.

Fortunately, as humans, we have many other alternatives for dressing warmly in the winter, like choosing clothes made of natural plant fibers, for example.

Alpaca fiber, is it ethical?

Get ready for some greenwashing:

"Alpaca fibers have been gaining popularity in recent years as a more ethical and environmentally friendly alternative to traditional wool. Unlike wool, which is obtained from sheep that are often subject to cruel practices like mulesing, alpaca fibers are obtained through gentle shearing of the animals, which is done once a year."

This sound beautiful, and we can often hear brands using alpaca as a "more ethical" alternative to wool, however, the truth is (unfortunately) the complete opposite…

Like all animals used to make clothes and accessories, **the fashion industry also tortures and mistreats alpacas.**

PETA's undercover investigation has uncovered appalling and inhumane treatment of alpacas at Mallkini, the world's largest privately owned alpaca farm near Muñani, Peru[1].

Workers were caught on camera kicking, hitting, and tying down pregnant alpacas that were crying in agony. The farm is owned by the world's biggest exporter of alpaca and a supplier of major brands.

The disturbing footage shows workers using excessive force and restraints that caused injuries, dislocations, and fractures to the alpacas. The animals were even mutilated and left bleeding from deep wounds. The alpacas' cries of distress and agony were ignored, and their instinct to flee from danger and potential harm was disregarded.

The alpaca fiber industry cannot be considered ethical as it subjects the animals to torture and mistreatment.

Both wool and alpaca fiber production involves

significant water requirements throughout various stages.

Firstly, raising these animals necessitates the use of drinkable water for their hydration. Additionally, water is essential for cultivating the crops that serve as their food source. Furthermore, the process of washing wool also demands water usage.

A study by Professor Wayne Meyer[2], sheds light on the astonishing water requirements involved in wool production. According to his research, a staggering 170,000 liters of water are consumed to produce a mere 1 kilogram of clean wool.

This eye-opening statistic underscores the significant impact on water resources that the wool industry entails. Considering the substantial water footprint associated with wool and alpaca fiber, exploring and embracing sustainable alternatives is imperative.

What is cashmere? Is it ethical?

Like traditional sheep's wool, cashmere comes directly from the "hair" made by a certain type of goat (cashmere goats) during the winter to protect itself from the cold.

Unlike traditional sheep's wool, cashmere grows less "hair." A single sheep can yield up to three kilograms of wool annually, whereas a goat typically produces only two hundred grams.

The harvesting is done directly on the animals (alive) by hand with an adapted comb. **The cashmere fiber is so fine that it takes around four goats to make only one sweater while it only takes one sheep to produce enough wool for five sweaters**[1]... which explains the very high price of cashmere products.

With a significant increase in the demand for cashmere products, the fashion industry saw a huge potential business... and therefore decided to industrialize the production of cashmere.

Obviously, "industrializing" means abandoning all moral, ethical and respectful rules. In order to produce more to sell more, the fashion industry has multiplied the number of goats per pasture, which now live in poor conditions and are malnourished. Moreover, this type of selectively bred "cashmere goat" eats all the plants and grasses down to the roots, leaving behind them completely deserted land with no vegetation left[2].

A normal and manageable phenomenon when kept on a "natural" scale, but it becomes much more serious when the fashion industry (to produce and sell more cashmere) introduces more and more goats into the pastures.

Harvesting is also industrialized and leads today to numerous animal mistreatments "to go faster."

Similar to the wool industry, numerous investigations[3] have revealed unethical practices within the cashmere industry. China and Mongolia, collectively accounting for 90 percent of global cashmere production, have been scrutinized.

PETA's disturbing footage[4] exposed goats experiencing distress as their hair was forcibly torn out before being slaughtered. The mistreatment of goats was found across farms in both China and Mongolia.

Furthermore, according to the United Nation Development Programme, Mongolia has witnessed 65%[5] degradation of its grasslands, with 90% of the country at risk of desertification, resulting in intense dust storms and air pollution.

Cashmere is often promoted as a natural product, however, once treated with many toxic chemicals, dyes... its biodegradability is hindered.

I'm not going to leave you like that!

The good news is that there are plenty of alternatives! If you are a fashionista at heart and you can't do without a touch of cashmere in your wardrobe, there are plenty of ethical (and vegan) materials that perfectly reproduce the cashmere effect, such as bamboo, tencel, modal, viscose, organic cotton and even soy cashmere, a co-product directly from the soy-based food industry.

Rats in my clothes?

It's a common nightmare: wearing clothes that are infested with rats. But what if that wasn't just a bad dream but a reality?

In Rome, police seized over a million items of counterfeit clothing, including coats and sweaters that were made from a mixture of "acrylic, viscose, and **fur from rats and other animals.**"[1]

While many people might not think twice about buying a knockoff designer sweater or coat, the reality is that clothing can be made from some pretty disturbing materials. In this case, counterfeiters were using the fur from rats and other animals to make clothing that was sold as cashmere. The items were seized by police, but it's unclear how many people may have already purchased these products and is now unknowingly wearing clothing that contains rat fur.

The issue of counterfeit clothing is not a new one, and it's not limited to Italy. In fact, fake designer clothing is a global problem that affects both consumers and legitimate fashion companies. In addition to the use of unsavory materials like rat fur, counterfeit clothing is often made under terrible conditions, with workers paid very little (if paid) and working in unsafe environments.

Just like we previously saw with cats' and dogs' leather, what is the difference between rat fur and goat hair?

Down, is it ethical?

The down industry has long been associated with comfort and luxury, providing soft, fluffy materials for clothing, bedding, and other products. However, what many people do not realize is that the production of down often involves a cruel and heartless practice called live plucking, where geese are plucked for their down while they are still alive.

Undercover video footage has revealed the brutal reality of live plucking on goose farms[1], where employees forcefully pull fistfuls of feathers out of live birds, causing them intense pain and trauma. These frightened animals are often held upside down between the workers' knees during the painful procedure, while some workers even sit on the geese's necks to prevent them from escaping.

Live plucking causes severe harm to the birds, leaving them with gaping wounds, some of which can be fatal. Workers often sew the birds' skin back together without using any anesthetics, further adding to their suffering.

Not only is live plucking inhumane, but it can also support the cruelty of the foie gras and meat industries.

During a PETA investigation, a farm openly acknowledged the annual production of a staggering 15 tonnes of live-plucked down, equating to an astonishing **250,000 instances of live plucking each year.**

Although down itself may have biodegradable properties, feathers are typically enclosed within jackets, coats, and sleeping bags, and the outer shell of these garments is commonly composed of non-biodegradable materials. This synthetic fabric serves as a protective barrier between the down insulation and the external environment, hindering its ability to biodegrade effectively.

However, there is hope for more ethical alternatives. As consumers become more aware of the cruel practices associated with down production, companies are beginning to offer alternatives that are sustainable and cruelty-free, made from 100% recycled and environmentally friendly fibers that are also biodegradable and disappear within a few years, unlike conventional non-biodegradable polymer fibers, which represent additional waste from the fashion industry.

Why silk is so bad for the planet?

Ah, silk! The luxurious, shiny, and oh-so-soft material that makes us feel like royalty. But hold on, before you drape yourself in a silk scarf, let's take a closer look at where it comes from.

Silk is created from the cocoons spun by some lucky caterpillars (Well, there you go…already not that great..). And while you probably love the end result, the journey from cocoon to fabric is not always a walk in the park for the environment.

First of all, it is necessary to go through several washing and sterilization processes, resulting in high water consumption… and, therefore, high-water pollution (much more important than for the production of synthetic fiber fabrics such as polyester or viscose).

Then, to give it its legendary supple and shiny appearance, the silk must be softened and "varnished" with numerous chemicals.

But it is not even these stages of silk production that have the worst impact on the environment. The real environmental impact of silk production is not just in the fabric-making process. The energy consumption required to raise the silk caterpillars is what really takes the cake (which makes it one of the most polluting fabrics, just after leather).

You see, creating a tropical paradise for these little guys requires heating and air-conditioning systems, and all that energy use adds up.

Lastly, we need to take into consideration the ethical behind silk. Researchers[1] have discovered that earthworms produce two types of chemicals, namely enkephalins and beta-endorphins, which exhibit similarities to opiates found in the human brain. These chemicals have the capacity to influence sensations of pleasure and pain. It is believed that the production of these substances by earthworms during the process serves as a mechanism to aid them in enduring painful experiences.

So, what's the verdict? While silk may look and feel amazing (or not), it's not exactly a friend to the environment, and it's not exactly kind to the caterpillars either.

But don't worry, because I do not like ending on a sad note, I have some good news!

Modern times have brought us alternatives to silk that are just as beautiful and even better for the planet. We're talking about silk made from bananas, lotus, and even synthetic fibers like spider silk (made from sugar, yeast, and water - no spiders were harmed in the making of this fabric!)

So, next time you're shopping for a silky-soft material, consider the journey it took to get to you and the impact it had on the environment. With so many amazing alternatives available, it's easy to make a choice that's good for both you and the planet.

FACT

It takes around 2,500 silkworms to produce one pound of raw silk[2]

Are pearls ethical?

"The truth behind pearls" would have been a perfect title for this question, but then it wouldn't be a question, so it had no relation to the concept of the book... Anyway!

Because it is a natural product and often associated with pretty thoughts (treasure, luck, rarity...) we tend to adore in good conscience this luxury "product".

However, the truth behind the production of pearls is much less poetic...

Pearls, naturally produced by mollusks and mainly oysters, are actually created by these animals in response to the stress caused when a parasite enters the oyster (a bit like when a human "creates" a nice ulcer caused by a major stress).

Ultimately, offering or wearing a nice oyster ulcer necklace to say I love you is less sexy...

In order to produce more pearls than the quantity we would usually find in the nature, industries and farmers have found a way to voluntarily stress the mollusks or to methodically insert parasites so that in response, by the defense, beautiful pearly pearls are produced.

This method, called "culturing" (#greenwashing) allows to produce pearls faster.

The reality is that, in the nature, only **one out of 10,000 oysters can form pearls**, and it can usually take up to three years for them to be produced[1].

The good news is that with this process, the animals are not killed, neither during the insertion of the parasite nor during the recovery of the pearl. Indeed, they are then simply plunged back into the water. To undergo the exact same process again. And again, and again, and again...

The REAL good news is that there are plenty of ethical and animal-friendly alternatives that mimic pearls to perfection.

Phew, we can continue to say I love you ;)

Fur will soon be banned worldwide, why not leather?

The global movement towards banning fur has gained significant momentum in recent years, with numerous countries and regions implementing legislation prohibiting fur farming and trade.

Disturbing undercover investigations[1] have revealed the cruel treatment of animals, such as foxes, minks, rabbits, coyotes, and others, who are trapped, confined, and killed in ways that inflict immense suffering, including gas and electrical methods to preserve the fur's integrity.

Many of these investigations were conducted in certified farms under the assurance scheme of SAGA Furs, which claims to uphold "the highest level of animal welfare."

Just like leather, fur undergoes extensive chemical treatment, including the use of harmful substances[2] like formaldehyde (linked to leukemia), chromium (linked to cancer), ammonia, and many more. These chemicals are employed to prevent decay and maintain the fur's desired texture, softness, and colorfulness.

In a study commissioned by ACTAsia, independent laboratories[3] have discovered dangerous levels of toxins in fur trims on children's fashion wear from well-known brands. The products were found to contain formaldehyde, which can cause allergies and cancer, and two out of six items contained Chromium 6 (see "What is Chromium,").

Dr. Jacob de Boer[3], a Professor of Environmental Chemistry and Toxicology at the Vrije University of Amsterdam says: "The alarming levels of toxics found in the fur trims of infant jackets and fur accessories in Europe and China justify stringent measures to seriously limit or prohibit the use of these chemicals in the preparation of fur products during production processes."

According to the Fur Free Alliance[4], there is currently no responsible authoritative body overseeing the monitoring of hazardous chemicals in fur products, ensuring compliance with regulatory benchmarks, and enforcing maximum levels set by industry standards

Due to the atrocious treatment and unnecessary killing of animals, several countries, including Austria, Croatia, the Czech Republic, Slovenia, and the Netherlands, have enacted legal bans on fur farming, effectively ending these breeding practices.

This trend has been mirrored in other nations such as Belgium, Norway, Slovakia, Estonia, Ireland, and Latvia, where fur farming bans have been announced or implemented, indicating a shift towards cruelty-free practices.

In 2021 Israel banned the sale of fur, followed by California. These bans are just the beginning of a natural movement, and the time when people could proudly go out with a dead fox, mink, or cat on the shoulder will soon become a regrettable memory.

Fortunately, numerous fur-free alternatives are emerging. For instance, Ecopel[5] has developed a biodegradable faux-fur that can be commercially composted within 180 days.

However, as fur faces increasing scrutiny and bans, why has leather, which shares similarities with fur, not faced similar widespread condemnation and regulatory action?

When you think about it, leather is nothing more than hairless fur.

Some might argue that animals used for fur, like minks, coyotes, and foxes, are not consumed as food, so fur isn't a by-product.

But we've already established that leather isn't a by-product either (see question "is leather a by-product of the meat industry?").

So, what is the justification now?

Shouldn't we advocate for a ban on leather with the same determination as we are pushing for the ban on fur?

To end on a positive note, a report by Marijn Bijleveld[6] concludes that the environmental impact of faux fur alternatives is significantly lower than that of real fur coats and trims. *(see below)*

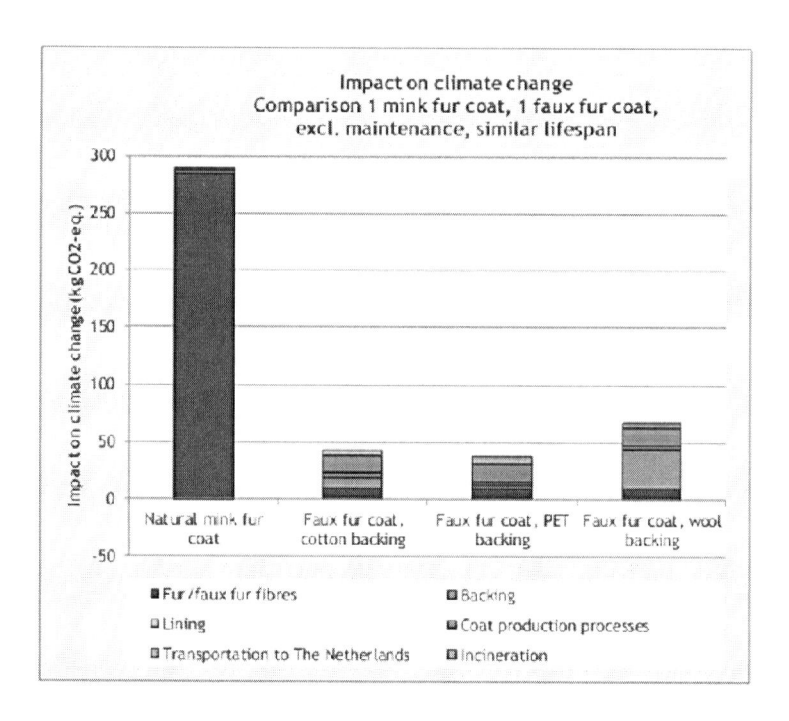

Second-hand leather, is it considered Vegan?

No.

"But it's not the same; the damage is already done!" (Yes, and that was, actually, the problem)

But wearing leather, even secondhand, is still promoting the idea, the "example" that animals are products, objects, and that we can still take advantage of them. Buying secondhand leather in thrift shops, vintage stores, markets, dedicated mobile apps etc... is continuing to "create demand" for leather products, as well as sending the message that we want more and more... thus encouraging the industries to (kill) produce more and more. #ThatsNotWhatWeWant

Imagine wearing a t-shirt that promotes a message that goes against your values. Even if this t-shirt was ethically made with organic fiber, I bet you wouldn't wear it.

Animal welfare in fashion, what is it?

Animal welfare is a crucial aspect of ethical responsibility, focusing on ensuring the well-being and humane treatment of animals. It encompasses several dimensions, including the physical, mental, and emotional state of animals, with the ultimate goal of minimizing or eradicating their suffering.

It is crucial to understand the distinction between animal rights and animal welfare.

Animal rights advocates for legal protections that grant animals with rights similar to those of humans; such as the right to life, freedom from exploitation, freedom from cruelty and abuse etc. This view also thinks people should not use animals for food, clothes, tests, or fun. It's about treating animals as friends, not as things we can use.

Animal Welfare is more about making sure that if animals are used by people—for example, as pets, on farms, or in science experiments—they are treated nicely and not hurt. This view says it's okay to use animals for human needs, but we should make sure they are comfortable, safe, and not suffering.

So, the main difference is: **Animal Rights** says "Don't use animals at all," while **Animal Welfare** says "If you're going to use animals, do it in a kind way."

The concept of animal welfare encompasses a range of considerations, including but not limited to the following:

Basic needs: Animals should have access to essentials such as food, water, shelter, and an environment that allows them to exhibit natural behaviors and avoid unnecessary suffering.

Health care: Animals should receive appropriate veterinary care to prevent and treat diseases, injuries, and pain, ensuring their overall well-being.

Freedom from discomfort: Animals should be kept in conditions that minimize physical and environmental discomfort, including extremes of temperature, overcrowding, or inadequate living spaces.

Freedom from pain, injury, or disease: Animals should be protected from physical harm, including deliberate cruelty, unnecessary procedures, and practices that cause distress or harm.

Freedom from fear and distress: Animals should not experience mental or emotional suffering due to fear, anxiety, or stress caused by their environment, handling, or interactions with humans.

Social interaction: Animals that have social needs should be allowed to interact with others of their species or suitable alternatives to fulfill their social requirements.

Animal welfare applies to various contexts, such as agriculture, research, entertainment, companion animals, wildlife conservation, and animal testing. It involves the establishment and enforcement of regulations, the development of standards and guidelines, the promotion of education and awareness, and the advocacy for the humane treatment of animals.

In the realm of fashion, we often encounter discussions about animal welfare in relation to cosmetics (ensuring they are not tested on animals) and animal-derived products like leather, fur, silk, and wool. However, it is important to note that the fashion industry generally lacks a genuine commitment to animal welfare. The inherent nature of fashion, which commodifies and exploits animals for profit, contradicts the fundamental principles of true animal welfare.

Tracing the origins of animal products in the fashion industry is exceedingly challenging, making it difficult to ensure ethical animal welfare practices. A piece of leather, for example, can easily originate from a source with questionable animal welfare standards, yet obtaining concrete proof of such conditions can be a complex and arduous process.

While many brands may claim to have an "animal welfare policy," a significant portion of these statements are often filled with greenwashing. This further highlights the lack of genuine concern for animal welfare within the fashion industry.

Ultimately, regardless of how animals are raised or killed for fashion purposes, the undeniable truth remains that their well-being cannot be achieved once they have been killed.

FACT

Animal welfare cannot exist for dead animals, as their well-being has been irreversibly compromised, highlighting the inherent contradiction in associating animal welfare with fashion.

HUMANS

in fashion

What is a "sweatshop"?

"Sweatshops" or "sweatshop factories" are manufacturing facilities that house hundreds of workers every day... where the work is simply illegal. Often overcrowded, the "working" conditions in the sweatshops are deplorable, dangerous for health and the environment, and show no humanity.

According to the US Department of Labor[1], a "sweatshop" is a term used to describe **a business that regularly violates two or more labor laws**, including both safety or health regulations, and wage or child labor laws.

The recruiters of these misery factories claim that they prefer to exploit children who are "more obedient and less complaining" than adults.

Obviously, the working hours are endless, well beyond the maximum allowed, and are in exchange for a derisory "salary" (if any). Many fashion industries use cheaper sweatshops to produce their products at lower costs.

Additionally, factories with certifications may use subcontractors, and it can be challenging to determine if these sub-contractors follow regulations and adhere to social laws, or they might be, in fact, very well-hidden sweatshops.

One of the most prominent examples we could give on sweatshops that you probably heard over the recent years (and if you haven't you should probably check it out) is the collapse of the Rana Plaza building in Bangladesh in 2013, killing at least 1,134 workers and leaving many more injured.

Then how can we be sure to avoid buying from a brand that uses sweatshop factories?

The most straightforward answer is that all fast-fashion companies use subcontracting businesses... So, we can make our own logical answer from that.

But to ensure we are on the right path to more ethical shopping, there is nothing better than local, 100% transparent, and honest designers and brands that care to produce ethically.

> *"There is no beauty in the finest cloth if it makes hunger and unhappiness."*
>
> **-Mahatma Gandhi**

What is "Rana Plaza" and what happened there?

In April 2013, one of the worst industrial disasters in history shook the fashion industry to its core. The Rana Plaza, a garment factory in Bangladesh, collapsed, **killing over 1,100 people and injuring more than 2,500[1].**

The factory was located in a multi-story building that housed five garment factories, a bank, and a few shops. This complex, located in Savar, Bangladesh, served as a manufacturing hub for several renowned global fashion brands. The majority of the 5,000 workers trapped within its walls were young women.

Despite visible structural cracks, factory workers were ordered to return to work the day after the building was evacuated due to safety concerns.

Tragically, the building collapsed just hours later, trapping thousands of workers inside. Survivors described the moment as a "big explosion". Many were forced to endure days of darkness, heat, and hunger before they were finally rescued.

The Rana Plaza disaster shed light on the terrible conditions that garment workers in Bangladesh and other developing countries face. Workers were paid very little, often working long hours in unsafe and unsanitary conditions. The Rana Plaza factory produced clothes for major fashion brands, and the tragedy exposed the industry's lack of accountability and transparency in its supply chains.

The disaster sparked a global outcry and demands for change in the fashion industry.

The Bangladeshi government and global brands

were pressured to improve safety standards and working conditions in factories.

The Fashion Revolution movement, commonly associated with the slogan "Who Made My Clothes?" emerged in the aftermath of the Rana Plaza tragedy, seeking to transform the fashion industry by encouraging consumers to question the origins of their garments and demand transparency regarding the conditions in which they are produced.

Today, the fashion industry still faces many challenges, including workers exploitation and environmental destruction. However, the tragedy brought much-needed attention to these issues and has led to a growing movement for a more sustainable and ethical fashion industry.

As consumers, we have the power to demand change in the fashion industry. By asking brands about their manufacturing processes and supporting sustainable and ethical fashion, we can make a difference and help prevent tragedies, like the Rana Plaza collapse, from happening again.

What does "handmade" means?

When a product is said to be handmade, it means that it has been produced by a worker with the use of their hands, **either by hand-sewing or even by machine-sewing**, as long as there is contact between the machine and the worker, and it's not a machine doing all the work on its own.

And for many reasons (work, expertise, technique, art, authenticity...), many of us appreciate the quality of a handmade product.

However, the handmade appellation is an unregulated, uncontrolled, non-certified appellation... and therefore widely distorted, exaggerated, or misused by some controversial companies, which thus use this appellation (and all the supposed values that go with it) to sell more... even if it's not totally true #Greenwashing.

By being aware of this practice, we quickly realize that depending on the brand, "handmade" is not necessarily ethical and can mean "handmade by a child exploited on the other side of the world".

Moreover, in front of the numerous industries that lower the market price through ethically questionable processes, real handmade work is threatened a little more each day. Textile arts, artisanal weaving techniques, and natural dyes are lost, with creators disappearing, swallowed up by the giants of fashion.

The good news is that it is possible to act easily, for each of us, on a daily basis while enjoying ourselves.

How do you do it? Simply by choosing to consume real handmade products and to be sure not to be fooled, we adopt the right reflexes by asking ourselves the right questions: where does the product come from? Are the working conditions supervised in this country? What is the price of the product? (Without being expensive, the true "handmade", which remunerates the creator in an ethical way, cannot be cheap).

If in doubt, check directly with the brand; with internet and social networks, most designers are happy to share their creative process!

To go even further, you can also opt for the so-called "artisanal" products, which means when a brand or atelier is producing unique products, hand-crafted in a traditional way made by a person skilled in these techniques.

Is the "minimum wage" ethical?

According to the latest data, the monthly minimum wage for garment workers around the world varies wildly. We're talking everything from a measly $26 a month in Ethiopia to a whopping $1,764 a month in Belgium (2018-2019)[1]. That's right, folks, the difference is enormous!

But before we go any further, let's talk about something called the "living wage." It's defined as the theoretical income level that an individual needs to earn to pay for basic essentials like shelter, food, and water in the country where they live[2].

As you might have guessed, a high minimum wage doesn't always translate to a high standard of living, and a small minimum wage doesn't necessarily mean a low living wage.

For example, in Ethiopia, where the minimum wage for garment workers is only $26 per month, it represent just 19% of the minimum living wage[1].

WHY?

Because when governments set the prices of the minimum wages allowed, they often encounter pressure from companies to keep wages low and remain competitive in the global market. As a result, they may not base their decisions on the calculations of the prices and costs of the essential needs of human beings to live in dignity. (yet it would seem logical to calculate like that…).

But, in reality, the price of mandated minimum wages is often based on... the global world market price of "labor" for fashion industry workers[3]... and thus calculate the cost of the mandated minimum wage to remain "cheap" and "attractive".

Yes, that's right... so the idea is to "sell off" the price of workers' lives.

Today the minimum wage allowed by governments for workers in the fashion industry is sometimes less than half of the average minimum wage estimated to allow a human being to meet basic needs and live in dignity. (We are talking here just about hygiene, food... not about going on vacations of course)

Always check where your garment are from and if the brand is (truly) transparent on their worker's conditions.

FACT

99% of major brands do not share the number of workers in their supply chains being paid a living wage*

*Fashion Revolution's Transparency index 2023

Modern slavery, is it really present in the fashion industry?

The CNN Freedom Project (a humanitarian media campaign to end modern slavery) refers to modern slavery as when: one person has total control over another person, using violence or threats of violence to maintain that control while exploiting them economically (by paying a very low income, or no income at all) so that the controlled person cannot leave.

So obviously, **YES, modern slavery is present in the fashion industry**; it is even very present.

To date, there needs to be more control, standards, and laws to regulate workers' conditions, especially in developing countries.

Whether it is in the fields during the cultivation of the raw material, at the harvest, at the multiple stages of transformation of the product, at the sending and the delivery, it is the whole chain of production of a garment that is maintained almost "secret", completely blurred... because it is perfectly illegal, and very far from the respect of the rights of men.

Despite numerous interventions and the growth of movements wishing to raise awareness about these practices and put an end to modern slavery, concrete governmental measures are still pending.

This does not prevent us from continuing every day to implement actions "at our level" to continue to fight and express our choices ... how? by choosing what we consume ... and what we no longer consume!

Because buying is voting!

"The fashion industry exploits children", is it true?

Yes.

According to the International Labour Organization (ILO), even if the numbers are slowly decreasing, **260 million children are "working" (exploited) around the world**[1]. Out of those, 170 million are considered to be in child labor, which is defined by the United Nations as work that is either performed by children below the minimum age requirement or work that is harmful and prohibited for children. Although child labor is illegal in most countries, it remains prevalent in some of the world's poorest regions.

Many of these children work (are exploited) in the fashion industries to meet the high demand to produce clothing for the European and American markets.

It is on the Asian continent that we find the most child labor (exploitation) (cotton production, crop harvesting, spinning, weaving, dyeing, pollination...). This is mainly due to the fact that there are almost no laws to regulate work and/or remuneration in Asia.

The origin of certain raw materials is often almost impossible to identify.

That's it. Unfortunately, a longer answer cannot be made here because it is an observation...

Here are some recommendations on how to address this issue:

- Asking to strengthen laws and regulations around child labor, especially in countries where it is prevalent, to prevent the exploitation of children in the fashion industry.

- Asking to increase awareness and education about the harmful effects of child labor.

- Encouraging fashion companies to be more transparent about their supply chains and to take responsibility for ensuring that no child labor is involved in the production of their products.

- Supporting initiatives and organizations that work towards ending child labor in the fashion industry and providing better working conditions and opportunities for children.

- Be more mindful of the products you purchase and support brands that are committed to ethical and sustainable practices.

What is MICA? And why is it so bad?

Mica is a natural mineral from the earth's crust (like iron, aluminum, or granite). Used in different civilizations for hundreds of years, nowadays it is mainly found in the tech (watches, smartphones) and beauty industries (in makeup for its shiny and pearly aspect).

Mica being a natural mineral, neither artificial nor man-made, if we stop writing this page here, we could almost say that everything is fine.

But,

The method of supply of mica is truly disastrous and very little information on the real working conditions of the workers. Most of these "workers" are young children, sent inside the mines, in extremely dangerous and illegal conditions.

Despite several investigations[1], the real employers of these workers remain unknown, which does not allow the situation to progress, leaving it without control or respect for ecological or social standards.

So, what can we do to not support this horrendous ingredient?

The best thing we can do is start asking questions and making our own research about mica and the brands that use it. While it's still difficult to find brands that are completely mica-free, we can look for brands that are either switching to synthetic mica or ethical mica, which means they're being more responsible with their sourcing of this ingredient.

So, let's spread the word and raise awareness about this issue. By making informed decisions and supporting responsible brands, we can help create a safer environment for the sourcing of mica. Together, we can create a more ethical and sustainable future.

List of things you can do to help protect these children and aid them:

- Support only ethical makeup brands.
- Supporting organizations aiding children from child labor.
- Pressure Beauty Brands to be more Ethical by asking them questions and more transparency.
- Share this information (you never know who you can impact).

Is it possible to be a feminist and buy fast fashion?

You spot it from across the store—the $3 fast fashion T-shirt adorned with a catchy pro-feminist message. In that instant, you're filled with a surge of excitement and a newfound sense of activism. It's time to rock that tee and spread the word about gender equality, right? But wait a minute, hold that thought! Before you embark on your mission as a self-proclaimed activist, let's take a closer look at the reality behind that seemingly empowering garment.

Digging beneath the surface, the International Labour Organization (ILO) reveals a stark reality. Women constitute nearly 60% of the global garment workforce, with some regions witnessing an astounding 80% female representation[1]. In particular, Asia is the largest garment sector employer, accounting for 75% of all workers. An estimated 42 million women toil away as garment workers in Asia alone.

What's more concerning is the dire circumstances these womens face. Many of these garment workers are **young women between 18 and 24, earning meager wages of less than $3 per day**[2]. This revelation shines a harsh light on the exploitation embedded within the fashion industry, often fueled by the insatiable demand for cheap, fast fashion.

The ILO's research also uncovers an average gender pay gap of approximately 18.5%[3]. Despite comprising most of the workforce, women consistently find themselves at a disadvantage regarding remuneration, perpetuating gender inequality within the industry.

Unfortunately, the issues plaguing the garment sector do not stop at unequal pay. Disturbing reports of sexual harassment have surfaced, exposing the vulnerability faced by women working in this field. The ILO survey conducted in Myanmar revealed that 42.5%[4] of women across 16 garment factories had experienced sexual harassment at work. A similar study by Better Work, titled "The Impact of Better Work"[5] showcased a grim reality in Indonesia, where **four out of five women workers reported sexual harassment** or unwelcome physical contact in their workplaces.

However, it is essential to acknowledge that violence and harassment are not the only forms of discrimination endured by these women. The industry's practices include invasive measures such as requiring women to undergo pregnancy tests during the hiring process[6]. Moreover, the devaluation of apparel jobs as "women's work" perpetuates a cycle of substandard labor conditions and diminished wages.

With all these sobering revelations, it becomes evident that purchasing a $3 fast fashion T-shirt with feminist slogans does little to address the systemic issues afflicting the garment sector. While these garments may give the illusion of support for gender equality, they do little to uplift the womens who create them.

True progress lies in recognizing the intricate challenges faced by garment workers, primarily women, and taking meaningful action to improve their working conditions and rights. Consumers can make a tangible difference by becoming more conscious of their purchasing habits, favoring brands that prioritize fair wages, safe working environments, and gender equality throughout their supply chains.

Simultaneously, fashion brands must take responsibility for the exploitative practices within their industry. They should implement transparent supply chains, invest in fair labor practices, and actively combat discrimination and harassment. By advocating for change and pushing for ethical standards, fashion brands can genuinely contribute to empowering the women who donate their skills and labor to the industry.

The $3 feminist T-shirt represents a paradox within the fashion industry. To truly support the feminist movement, we must shift our focus from superficial symbols to tangible actions that uplift the voices and rights of the very women who create our garments. Only then can we begin to dismantle the inequalities that persist in the world of fashion and strive for a more equitable future.

Boycotting fast fashion, do workers suffer from it?

Many people have chosen to boycott fast fashion brands in an effort to support ethical and sustainable fashion practices, but some have raised concerns that boycotting could harm the workers who rely on these jobs to support themselves and their families.

So, does boycotting fast fashion hurt the workers?

The short answer is no; boycotting fast fashion does not hurt the workers. In fact, it may be one of the most effective ways to improve the working conditions and wages of those who produce our clothes.

People often worry that if we stop buying from fast fashion companies, the workers who make those clothes might lose their jobs. They think it might be worse for those workers to have no job at all, even though the jobs they do have don't pay much, as long as it's something.

But that's neither the truth, nor the purpose of boycotting fast fashion. That kind of thinking is basically the excuse for not helping to make a change, or even worse, for having a "reason" of why people buy from sweatshops.

Fast fashion brands are notorious for exploiting workers in developing countries by paying them extremely low wages and subjecting them to poor working conditions. These workers often lack basic labor rights and are forced to work long hours in unsafe factories.

By continuing to support these brands, consumers are essentially condoning these unethical practices and perpetuating the cycle of exploitation.

Boycotting fast fashion sends a message to these

companies that their practices are not acceptable and that consumers demand change. When sales decrease, companies are forced to re-evaluate their practices and may be more likely to make changes to improve working conditions and wages. It also creates a demand for ethical and sustainable fashion, which can lead to the growth of new brands and the creation of new jobs that prioritize the well-being of workers and the environment.

It is important to acknowledge that simply boycotting fast fashion is not enough to solve the systemic issues of worker exploitation and environmental degradation. Consumers must also advocate for policy changes and support organizations that work to improve labor conditions and protect workers' rights. It is also crucial to support brands that prioritize ethical and sustainable practices and hold companies accountable for their actions.

Boycotting fast fashion does not hurt the workers but rather provides an opportunity to make a positive impact on their lives and the environment. By choosing to support ethical and sustainable fashion practices, consumers can send a powerful message to companies, that prioritize profits over people, and demand change.

FACT

As long as fast fashion exists, so will these work conditions.

What diseases "toxic" clothing can cause?

Due to the many chemicals that clothing contains, it is sometimes possible for people to develop illnesses as a reaction to wearing some types of clothing.

For example, leather jackets contain chromium (used for dyeing and tanning leather). This highly chemical product can cause skin reactions such as itching, redness, and blisters in people who wear these jackets.

For Jeans, azo dyes can be found in the dye, which can release amines (carcinogenic chemicals)[1].

Formaldehyde, which is often the cause of the "chemical smell" on new clothes, has been linked to numerous health issues, including asthma, nausea, cancer, and dermatitis.

These are just examples of all the many chemicals used in the Fashion industry.

Although no studies prove these chemicals can cause diseases, there's a concern that they could be toxic. Despite this, it's still worth considering choosing safer clothing options, especially when responsible (and stylish) alternatives are available.

How can your body absorb chemicals from "toxic" clothing?

Long before being a fashion statement or a way to express one's personality, the primary function of clothing is to cover our bodies and keep us warm.

This means that clothes and fabrics are in direct contact with our skin and our body all day and night...that's why it is interesting to choose them well and to pay attention to their "toxicity."

That is to say, pay attention to their origin and to the chemical products they may contain (harmful dyes or colorants, glues or chemical softeners, etc...)

During day and night, our body temperature changes, and even without doing a big workout, our pores dilate to promote sweating (even light sweating). This is when our skin can absorb (like when we apply moisturizer) the fine toxic and chemical particles from our clothes.

Although official figures and studies have not been published and are still a little unclear, this process has been proven... and it is a good reason (as if there was still a need for more reasons) to opt, without hesitation, for organic clothing, made from natural fibers.

Is wearing clothes also wearing values?

For centuries, what we choose to wear (or not to wear) was a way to express ourselves, to share our opinions, to gather, to prove our belonging to a social class...

Today in our current society, in the era of fast fashion and over consumption, even if our way of dressing is a "less marked" indicator than in the past (like in the Middle Ages for example), what we wear remains a result of our choices, of the clothes we choose to (or not to) buy.

So obviously, when we choose to wear brands known for exploiting workers, using harmful chemicals, mistreating animals, or any other unethical practices, especially when there are sustainable alternatives available, we're essentially endorsing these unsavory methods.

By wearing these products, we communicate our acceptance of the processes behind their creation and perpetuate such harmful industries....

So, yes.

Wearing clothes is also wearing values!

Does buying new clothes make us happy?

There is always that feeling of joy and adrenaline after purchasing an item, but does this mean that we have achieved happiness then?

Studies on the subject have proved that the general answer is NO.

Let's take the Easterlin paradox as an example. Research from 1974[1], named after its creator Richard Easterlin, focuses on the investigation of the impact of economic growth on the population's global happiness. Showing results that despite the formidable economic growth the United States experienced from 1946 to 1970, its population's happiness has remained stable, as if a **better purchasing power and life quality didn't conclude in a happiness rise**. Could it be possible that purchasing more wouldn't lead to being happier?

Buying something new is like a quick hit of happiness! We feel that surge of excitement and rush of adrenaline running throughout our veins as we reach for our wallets, making us think that we are happy, and we probably are, for just an instant.

But let's be real. That feeling is usually short-lived.

After the initial thrill wears off, we're often left with that shopping hangover, regretting the impulse purchase and feeling guilty about spending money on something we didn't really need.

In a 2017 article from Forbes[2], they talked about this instant gratification and how the quest for any consumer is to feel satisfied and to feel it now and that we are wrongly looking for that gratification in materials when we should be looking for it in more deep and meaningful ways, because, at the end, **materials don't lead us to achieve a greater personal fulfilling.**

The article mentions a study as well from Professor Marsha Richings, from the University of Missouri, named "When wanting is better than having". Basically, our emotions increase before making a purchase rather than during or after. Take online shopping for an instance, the shopping is easy, just one click and we're all good, but before that click we have the research, we could spend hours looking for the perfect product to get, putting all our attention into getting it and hoping it would be the perfect fit, and when we finally find it and make the purchase, there's the waiting time until its physically ours, but it's that waiting that makes us feel more excited, we daydream about it, counting the days until we get to have it in our hands.

Marketing clearly doesn't help us to stop it but actually encourages us to shop more; we see ads everywhere, on the streets, the metro, on TV, and on our phones. In today's world, it's all about consumerism, and their approach is to make us think that we are going to be as joyful as the models posing for their publicity advertisements, but the reality is that it is all a fantasy, a dream created by the big corporations, by psychologically playing with our minds, and we fall into them.

These advertisements cleverly use mannequins and models with idealized body types—skinny, muscular, and beyond— This tactic cleverly exploits our insecurities, making us believe that attaining these beauty standards is just a purchase away. It's a manipulative play, convincing us that perfection is a commodity sold by corporations, pushing us into an endless cycle of consumption in the pursuit of an ideal that, in reality, doesn't exist.

So how do we stop the obsessive shopping?

Firstly, we need to understand how this circle has been created.

Emotions are the major triggers that lead us to shop, and brands know how to play this game because it's all about them; they don't actually sell a product, they sell a feeling. We, in fact, consume more than what we need and thinking about it in a sustainable way, the planet cannot keep affording that kind of consumerism. More demand requires more production, which eventually leads to pollution and waste, and the fashion industry is considered the second largest polluter in the world.

Do you actually want to feel happy when shopping? Do it consciously.

Clothing is a human necessity, but don't shop out of anxiety, do it out of pleasure and find, within that pleasure, the satisfaction of helping the planet with the way you consume. Ethically shopping it's not just about you, it's about the brand, the workers, the planet, and the animals!

True happiness is not something that you own, it's something that you are.

FACT

Happiness is a choice...
Choose wisely.

Could fashion have an impact on our mental health?

Psychology does play a role when it comes to the choices of our clothing. Very regularly, you don't choose an outfit or color randomly. In fact, how you dress affects your mood, and how you feel affects your choices of outfits… it works both ways.

In her book "*Mind what you wear the psychology of fashion*" by Professor Karen Pine[1], she combines her knowledge of fashion with psychological theories studied to understand why people wear what they wear. She describes how your personality affects and is affected by your wardrobe; choosing the right outfit might lead you to life-changing decisions or how when you're dressed down it can make you feel like hiding and being transparent.

In her research, professor Pine asked 100 women what they wore when feeling depressed. The results were that 57% of them would wear baggy pants or jeans when depressed. Only 2% of those women would wear those outfits when happy.

The research also revealed that 67% of the women would use their favourite dresses when happy and only 6% when depressed.

According to the psychology of fashion, **clothes speak to people**. And it works like attraction, when you have positive thoughts, you attract positive, but when you have negative thoughts, well guess what you attract.

"Dress to kill" exists for a reason, so when you feel powerful, you wear something that matches that state of mind, and your confidence increases.

On the other hand, when you're feeling down, it's expected that all you want to do is wear comfy clothes such as sweatpants and while that is completely ok, it's also ok to try to cheer yourself up by wearing something that you love entirely, to try to put you in a better mood.

It's not about changing who we are and acting like a different person (or at least it shouldn't), it's about giving ourselves a boost, like a pep talk, to embrace ourselves, to cheer us up, to be inspired, and clothing can have that exact effect.

Enclothed cognition[2] is a term introduced by Hajo Adam and Adam D. Galinsky that illustrates that clothing impacts human cognition based on two primary concepts, the symbolic meaning of the clothes and the physical experience of wearing them.

To get answers to this term, they made a few experiments that involved a group of people being assigned to certain activities while wearing a doctor's coat, a painter's coat and wearing no coat but seeing a doctor's coat in front of them while performing the activity. The results were that the participants had a higher level of attention and performed better while wearing a doctor's coat; this was also affected when the participants learned they were wearing a doctor's coat, proving that not only by the physical experience of wearing a piece of clothing can psychologically affect you but also by knowing the importance of such clothing.

It has been known that color can also affect our moods; if you ever felt certain emotions or moods depending on the colors of the rooms you were in, that could be the reason.

It has also been known that color can help with both psychical and mental health improvement. Chromotherapy is an ancient alternative medicine that has been used to improve and cure different types of illnesses by using light in form of colours to balance the energy of a person's body.

The meanings that one can give to colors can be subjective, based on personal experiences and cultures. But in general research colors had been associated to different types of meanings such as:

-**White:** Innocence, purity, goodness.
-**Yellow:** happiness, hope, joy, optimism, vitality.
-**Orange:** Energy, ambition, extroversion.
-**Pink:** Love, romance, inspiration.
-**Red:** Confidence, stimulation, power, passion.
-**Brown:** Natural, stability, reliable.
-**Purple:** Creativity, luxury, royalty.
-**Green:** Balance, prosperity, growth.
-**Blue:** Serenity, intelligence, trust.
-**Black:** Strength, elegance, protection.

Depending on our mood or even the activity we would realize, we choose the colors we think might work for that precise moment, and that can either affect how we feel or what we want to project to others.

It is so important, **when choosing the right outfit, to choose one that balances our moods as well as our values**. Wearing something that we know can do good to other people, the planet, and the animals, by respecting them and not using them for our own purposes. This can make us feel better and improve our mental health and, with that, our physical one.

Although an individual's wardrobe can provide a temporary boost during low moments, it is essential to seek professional guidance for any serious physical or mental illnesses.

No disease can simply disappear on its own and requires proper treatment, but in the meantime, we can always count on our wardrobes to boost ourselves up and shine!

PRODUCTION

and its environmental impact

How many clothes are made each year?

Guessing how many new clothes get made each year is like trying to count the stars from your backyard – a fun but pretty impossible task! With fashion trends changing faster than a chameleon, who can keep up?

So, How many clothes are made each year?

Estimates vary anywhere between **80 and 150 billion garments every year**[1]. **That's between 220 million and 410 million clothes PER DAY!**

This number gap highlights a significant challenge within the fashion world: **there is a desperate need for more clear and transparent information.** Most of these estimates don't even have strong proof or data to back them up.

Fast fashion is at the forefront of this problem. Garment production has exploded due to the cultural rush toward ultra-cheap, disposable fashion. That's a whole lot of fabric, dye, and other resources being used up to create clothes that many of us will only wear a few times before tossing them aside.

Lack of transparency from brands is one big headache in getting accurate data. Surprisingly, in 2023, around **88% of the most major brands did not publish annual production figures**[2]. This opacity is an essential obstacle in understanding production's actual scale and environmental impact.

The need for reliable data has never been more urgent. However, Fashion Revolution's Transparency Index 2023 states that "99% of fashion brands do not disclose a commitment to reduce the number of new items they produce".

But it doesn't stop there...

On top of all the new clothes being produced, the industry also generates an incredible amount of waste. **Each year, people discard textiles exceeding a value of $450 billion[3]. Less than 1% of material used to create clothing are being recycled into new garments[4].**

Most of these materials end up in landfills (over 90 million tons a year[5]), which take decades or even centuries to decompose. Waste not only represents a loss of resources but also creates environmental pollution.

The good news is that by thoughtfully choosing and wearing our clothes, thinking about where they came from and how it affects nature around us, we can be inspired to make better choices, and significantly reduce our impact on the environment.

Opting for second-hand clothing or reusing existing ones reduces the demand for new clothing production and prevents excess materials from being discarded.

It may seem like a small step, but every little bit counts.

It's (almost) as if a truck filled with clothes is dumped onto a landfill site every second.

Is 'made in Europe' or 'made in USA' necessarily ethical?

"Made in Europe" or "Made in USA" suggests that the product was manufactured in a specific region, but this alone doesn't provide a comprehensive understanding of its ethical standing.

Made in Europe doesn't mean made in a small ethical and luxurious workshop in the middle of Paris.

Both Europe and the USA have stringent labor laws, ensuring minimum wages, worker safety, and prohibiting child labor. However, exceptions and lapses do occur, meaning not every product manufactured here upholds ideal labor practices.

For instance, before the introduction of the bill SB62 in 2022, nearly 45,000 garment makers were underpaid in California, receiving $5.85 an hour on average (and some as low as $1.58 an hour according to a report released by the U.S. Department of labor[1]). Crafting for major international brands, their compensation was tied to a "piece-rate system." This meant they were paid for each hem, seam, or cuff they sewed, with some pieces earning them a meager three cents for the whole item.

SB62 requires employers to pay an hourly wage and only allows piece-rate compensation as an incentive bonus. This bill was a huge step towards a more ethical fashion industry in California.

Even if a product boasts a "Made in Europe" or "Made in USA" label, its components might be sourced from countries with lower ethical standards. For example, a shirt sewn in the USA might use cotton harvested under questionable conditions elsewhere.

Furthermore, given the vast cultural diversity within Europe and the geographical expanse of the USA, it's an oversimplification to generalize ethical practices based on these labels. What might be a norm in one part might be an exception in another, making these labels an unreliable gauge of ethical consistency.

Though both regions have strict environmental regulations compared to some other parts of the world, the presence of an origin label doesn't automatically imply sustainability or eco-friendliness. Additionally, the environmental impact of transporting raw materials to these manufacturing hubs and then transporting finished products worldwide can't be ignored.

While the "Made in Europe" or "Made in USA" labels might evoke trust and quality for many, equating them directly with universally ethical practices can be an oversimplification. **These labels should be seen as starting points rather than conclusive evidence of ethical production.**

Ethical consumption requires a deeper understanding of products, their origin, and the practices behind them. Instead of relying solely on these labels, consumers can look for additional certifications, conduct research, or support brands known for their commitment to ethical standards.

$9.99 T-shirt, how is this price possible?

In stores, you can find clothes at all prices. Very very expensive, very expensive, expensive, fair price, cheap, very cheap, very very cheap.

How is such a price difference possible?

How do some brands manage to lower their prices so much?

Answer: Simply by reducing the only production cost that can be reduced... the remuneration of workers, the cost of "labor."

Ready for some math? Probably not, but I'll do my best, because it's still very important and interesting!

For the example of a T-Shirt at $9.99:

In the fast fashion industry, to make money on a freshly made product, a brand must resell this item at least 2.5 times more expensive than the factory purchase price.

So, for a T-Shirt sold at $9.99 in store, the factory price was certainly around $3.99

In this $3.99 factory price, we also find the margin of the factory, which sells to the brands at least 2.5 times more expensive than the production cost.

So, for a T-Shirt sold at $3.99 in a factory, the production cost was certainly $1.59

In these $1.59 of production cost, there is about $1 of raw material (which is impossible to reduce), plus $0,50 of transport (at its minimum) ...

If we did our math correctly, that means that for a T-shirt produced for $1.59, the workers' remuneration is approximately $0.09, the only possible cost that can be reduced.

So, the "good deal" of a T-Shirt at $9.99 is simply the good exploitation of a worker, paid $0.09.

To go a little further (because, in reality, I have a little taste for math), we estimate that a worker (exploited) takes about 20 minutes to produce a T-Shirt, that is to say, 3 T-shirts per hour, (3 x $0.09) = **$0.27 per hour.**

That's when the (lucky) worker gets paid (if he/she ever gets paid, because, yes, fast fashion is actually known to deprive the remuneration of workers claiming to not have the money to do so).

To put things in perspective, if you were getting paid that amount, you would have to work for four days to get one large vanilla latte (with dairy alternative of course) at a regular coffee shop.

It is essential to remember that this math is a generalized model; we cannot assume that every clothing business works the same way because every brand has its own business plan and own margins, and while most of the above information it's actually true within the fast fashion industry, it could also apply to some other non-fast fashion brands, but fortunately we can always find brands that are way more transparent and ethically fair within their margins and remunerations.

Luxury fashion, does expensive necessarily mean ethical?

Ah, luxury fashion. The epitome of glamour, sophistication, and style. From the exclusive fabrics and intricate designs to the impeccable craftsmanship, luxury fashion brands have always managed to create a sense of opulence that we all crave. But here's the million-dollar question: does a high price tag necessarily mean ethical?

Believe it or not, we tend to assume that expensive equals ethical because we think using organic or eco-friendly materials and paying workers fairly should come at a higher cost. However, that's not always the case. In fact, the luxury fashion industry is under fire for its ethical and environmental practices.

To begin with, the raw materials come from the same fields, cultivated by the same farmers. (#BreakingNews a cotton field is not divided in two with a part dedicated to fast fashion and a part dedicated to luxury fashion) so from this step the price difference is not justified by "a more qualified workforce for luxury clothes".

The myth of luxury fashion being hand-crafted by skilled artisans is only partly true. While it is true that luxury fashion brands employ skilled workers, the conditions in which they work are not always great. Reports of sweatshops and poor working conditions in luxury fashion factories are rife, and it's not just fast fashion that's guilty of this.

Sometimes, the exact same factories produce and deliver the cheap and luxury brands.

But wait, there's more! The materials used in luxury fashion are not always sustainable or ethical. The leather used in luxury bags and shoes often comes from animals raised in inhumane conditions, while the production of luxury fabrics like silk and cashmere can have serious environmental consequences, including deforestation, water pollution, and the use of toxic chemicals.

Now, before you go cancelling your high-end shopping sprees, there are some luxury fashion brands that prioritize ethics and sustainability. These brands use eco-friendly materials, implement fair labor practices, and are transparent about their supply chain. It's time to start paying attention to these brands.

As consumers, **we hold the power to influence the luxury fashion industry by choosing to support ethical and sustainable brands**. But let's not forget that the responsibility lies with the luxury fashion brands to step up their ethical and environmental game. By doing so, they not only benefit the planet and the people, but also enhance their reputation and appeal to conscious consumers.

In conclusion, while we may think that expensive means ethical in the luxury fashion industry, it's crucial to look beyond the marketing and consider the ethical and environmental implications of our choices. Let's create a more conscious and responsible fashion industry!

What happens to unsold clothes?

Clothes are often made really, really fast - faster than they can be sold. Many of these clothes don't get the chance to reach any wardrobe on time.

So where do they go?

Sadly, they often end up in giant trash piles or are burned up. It almost seems as if they go from being made, straight to being thrown away.

Let me repeat it for the people in the back: **Products that are still good to use are thrown away in landfills or goes to the incinerator instead of being sold at a discounted prices or donated!**

"**But...WHY?**" you may ask.

Well, many fast fashion and luxury brands decide to destroy their unsold clothes to "protect their brand" or, in better word, to "maintain brand value, high status, and exclusivity". As you can believe, destroying items that shouldn't have been produced in the first place, exacerbates the environmental issue the fashion industry is facing by releasing harmful gases into the atmosphere.

A representative from a luxury brand mentioned that they have strict methods to reduce the amount of extra products they make. When they need to get rid of products, they do it carefully and responsibly. They are also always looking for ways to decrease and find new uses for their waste[1].

#greenwashing?

They also explained their fear that the market could become flooded with discounts, which would devalue the brand.

While recycling seems like the obvious solution, it's not

as simple. Most clothes aren't designed for recycling, and the process can be cost-efficient. Different materials and dyes complicate recycling, often leading to lower quality products[2].

Brands also have financial incentives to destroy unsold items, such as avoiding inventory fees.

Some regions, like the European Union, are taking action against this wasteful practice. Proposed policies include banning the destruction of unsold textiles. But the change is gradual, and the entire system needs a redesign.

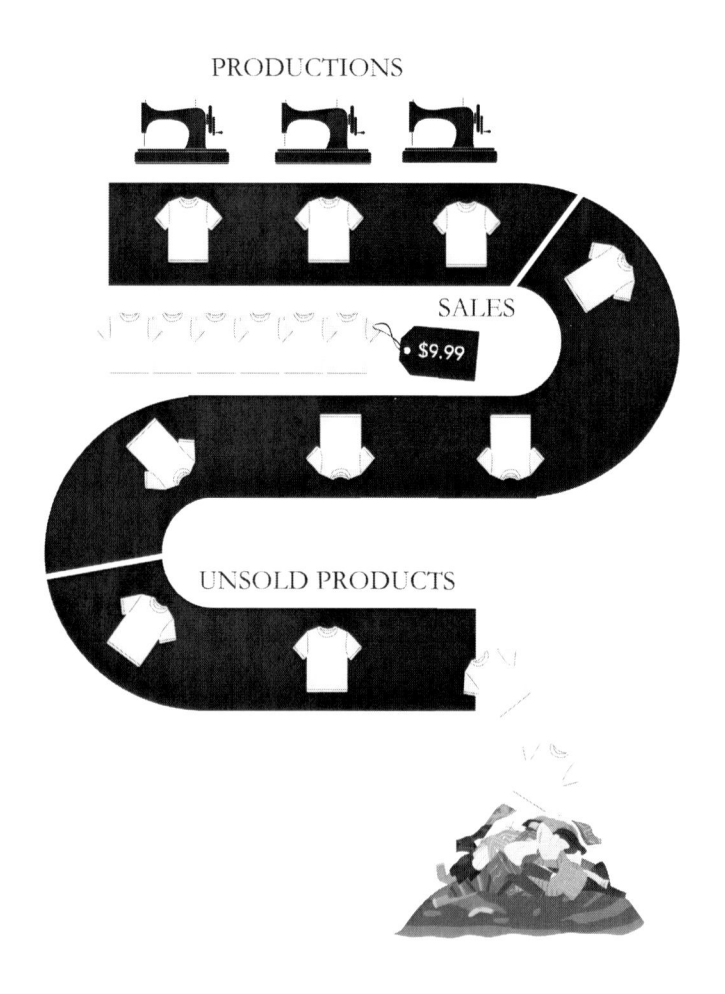

Is vegan fashion necessarily ethical, ecological, and responsible?

According to the meaning of veganism… They should be, but sadly they are not always.

If "vegan" means "cruelty-free" (and that's already very very very very good), in no way does vegan fashion guarantee respect for workers or the environment.

Even when most of the vegan creators turn to ecological and responsible products, (and that the fact that creating products respecting the animal welfare is already necessarily more ecological than classic production!) It happens that we can find, in the production of items that happened to be vegan, chemicals and toxic components bad for the planet, or the use of cheap labor, not necessarily ethical nor paid at the right price.

In the fast-fashion industry, we often come across "vegan" products that may actually be vegan (containing no animal products) but are likely loaded with toxins and plastic. In some cases, it is just a deceptive marketing claim. #GreenWashingOfCourse

But even if vegan fashion is not necessarily ethical or ecological, it is important to realize that responsible fashion, (which commits to ethical and environmentally friendly products), should always be vegan!

So while waiting for a fashion or a label which gathers all these nice values all together, let's continue to read the labels ;)

Microplastic, how much is released into the oceans by the fashion industry?

A IUCN study (International Union for the Conservation of Nature) conducted in 2017, shows that **34.8% of the microplastics found in the ocean originate from synthetic clothing**[1] (which represent between 200 000 and 500 000 tonnes of microplastics[2]).

How is this possible?

Roughly 60% of clothing and 70% of household textiles worldwide are composed of synthetic polymer-based fibers[3]. But you might be wondering how a t-shirt ends up as microplastics in our oceans

A report from the Institution of Mechanical Engineers reveals that, when we launder our clothes, approximately 700,000 microscopic fibers from synthetic fabrics are released into the oceans[4].

This is obviously disastrous for all marine life... and even for our lives since most of these microplastics end up directly in our food.

In fact, the International Marine litter research unit from the University of Plymouth discovered that a significant amount of microplastic contamination comes from plastic packaging and even synthetic rope, such as fishing nets; releasing around 20 microplastic fragments for every yard hauled in the ocean[5].

Researchers estimate that new rope can release up to 2,000 microplastic fragments with each use, while old rope could yield as many as 40,000 particles eventually breaking down and being eaten by small fish, that eventually big fish would eat and this way climbing up the food chain until arriving to humans.

What can we do about it?

First, if we want to save fish, the best way to do so would be to stop eating them, of course.

Second, moreover on the fashion note, we should also stop buying synthetic clothes and materials, because, for every wash that we do to our "polyester", "nylon", "polyamide", etc., we are releasing tiny plastic fibers directly into the ocean. At least if you wash clothes made with synthetic fiber, try to use a wash bag.

So, we should try to opt for more ecological and natural fibers to wear. It's good for the environment and good for our skin, so all in!

#ItsAWinWin

FACT

By using a filter in your washing machine, you can cut down the release of microfibers by a significant 80%[6]

Water, how much is wasted by the fashion industry?

In the world of fashion, water plays an indispensable role, serving as versatile resource that touches every aspect of the industry. From growing natural materials (such as cotton, hemp...) to bleaching and dyeing fabrics, spinning, washing, finishing, softening, and even printing... Water is like this one friend of your fashion item that you can't avoid.

A study called "the environmental price of fast fashion" conducted by Nature Reviews Earth & Environment in April 2020 states that **79 trillion liter of water is used every year for fashion**[1].

To give you a nice perspective, 79 trillion liter of water is enough water for 7 billion humans to drink for 9 year! (Yeah I calculate it myself).

This number is so high that it's almost impossible to imagine!

However, the study omits details about the water's origins, but the magnitude of the number remains undeniably significant.

Reducing water waste and promoting sustainability in the fashion industry is crucial, and there are many steps that can be taken toward achieving this goal.

One way is to support companies that use environmentally friendly methods of production, such as using organic fabrics or recycled materials. Consumers can also play a role by choosing to purchase second-hand clothing, which keeps clothes out of landfills and saves water and resources.

Additionally, using water-saving technologies in the production process and implementing better water management practices in garment factories can significantly reduce the amount of water used in production.

Finally, promoting awareness about the issue of water waste in the fashion industry, and encouraging consumers to make more informed choices, can help drive change toward a more sustainable future.

Certifications and labels, is it really reliable?

Yes and no.

Yes, the creation of certifications and labels starts from a good intention, that of wanting to "frame" the creation of products according to ethical, sustainable, environmentally friendly and animal welfare processes.

But (and it's kind of ironic when you think about it), the certifications a nd labels themselves are not very regulated. So today we find ourselves with dozens of different certifications, each promising nice things, but based only on their own criteria. Respect for workers, respect for nature, respect for animals... but rarely all at once, and always according to random standards.

In addition to having to learn by heart "which certification corresponds to which promise", it turns out that some brands, even though they got a certain certification for being eco-friendly or ethical, might still have parts of their products made by other companies (subcontractors) that don't follow those good practices. Thus indirectly derogating from the promises of the certification. #Greenwashing ?

So how do we know when and what to believe?
- Use certifications and labels as indicators rather than absolute truths.
- Ask directly to the brands!

Many designers make ethical, sustainable and respectful products but don't have certifications simply because they are not free... and expensive! And supporting small local brands instead of big industries is still pretty cool.

Is it ethical to donate your clothes?

Have you ever felt overwhelmed by the amount of clothes in your closet?

You're not alone!

In fact, between 1960 and 2018, the United States saw a big increase in the amount of textile waste, from 1.76 million tons to 17.03 million tons (10 times more). Despite more recycling, most of this waste (around 66%) still end up in landfills[1].

That's a lot of clothes! So what do you do with all those items that no longer fit or you simply don't wear anymore? You donate them, of course! But is donating your clothes really the ethical thing to do?

First of all, let's talk about what happens to your donated clothes. Many people donate their clothing to charity shops, such as Goodwill, with the hope that it will be resold and given to someone in need. However, the reality is that **95% of donated clothes are resold, while the remaining 5% are discarded** due to mildew issues[2].

Yes, many people think trash equals donation.

The rest of the clothes are put on display in Goodwill stores for four weeks and then sent to outlets where they are sold for 99 cents per pound. Items not purchased in outlet stores are then offered at Goodwill auctions. These are live bidding events where participants place offers on containers filled with donated goods, the exact contents of which are unknown to the bidders.

Finally, the leftover items will end up at the textile recycling centers.

Now, what happens to your clothes at the recycling

centers? Synthetic fibers, such as polyester, are processed to give them a new life (such as plastic pellets), while fibers like cotton or wool, are cleaned and re-spun into yards of threads. These recycled materials can be used to create new products, keeping them out of landfills and reducing the need for virgin fibers.

The recycling rate for all textiles in United States varies by source, but it is generally low. According to the U.S. Environmental Protection Agency (EPA), the recycling rate for all textiles was 14.7% in 2018, with 2.5 million tons recycled[3]. A report from the National Institute of Standards and Technology (NIST) also states that only about **15% of used clothes and other textiles in the United States get reused or recycled**[4].

This indicates that a significant portion of textiles end up in landfills or incinerators, contributing to waste and environmental pollution.

Another example is these major fast-fashion brands offering to accept your old clothes as donations. These brands propose to take your old clothes, assuring you that they will manage them responsibly and, in return, offer you a discount in their store.

Well, the development sustainability manager of one of these significant fast fashion brands shared that only 0.1% of all apparel collected by charities and their take-back programs is recycled into new textile fibers[5]. **#greenwashing?**

This revelation raises questions about the true nature of such an initiative. Is this offer a trap to encourage more spending and consumption in their stores, offering a sense of good conscience in exchange? I'll let you be the judge!

But here's where it gets interesting: **a lot of the**

secondhand clothing that doesn't sell in the US is exported to other countries. The EPA report roughly 700,000 tons of used clothing every year[3]! This is about 78,000 trailer trucks full of clothes sent overseas!

Some countries in Africa were getting a lot of secondhand clothes from the US. This influx of cheap, used garments was hurting the local clothing industries in those countries, and people were starting to rely more on imported clothing. Local artisans express their frustration about the necessity of lowering prices to stay in line with competing businesses and trying to survive[6].

A lot of the clothes that come from the U.S. aren't in good enough shape to be used. Sadly, they often end up being thrown away in landfills or just left in open areas. Some left over clothes are incinerated, releasing harmful gases and chemicals that dirty the air, ground, and water. This is not only harming the environment, but it also impacts the health of people and animals.

There's also a very big problem with these extra clothes blocking up the water drainage systems. This leads to more flooding and increases the chance of diseases that spread through water.

In 2016, the East African Community agreed to ban the import of used clothing, but the ban was eventually rescinded due to pressure from the US government[7].

This situation sparked a debate about whether it's better to support local textile industries or provide livelihoods through the secondary clothing market (selling second-hand clothes).

So, what's the ethical answer? Is it right to donate your clothes?

As you're scrolling through this page, I bet a couple of

questions are popping into your head. You might be thinking, "Hey, can I still hang on to these clothes or maybe give them a new life?" Or perhaps, "Was buying these clothes a mistake?"

It is very important to pause and think about this crucial moment in your clothes' journey. Imagine the point where you'll have to part ways with that shirt, those jeans, or the dress you're eyeing to buy. It's not about judging your choices as right or wrong. It's about being mindful and making decisions that you'll be at peace with later on.

The truth is, there's no straightforward answer. On one hand, donating clothes can help reduce waste and extend the life of existing fibers. On the other hand, it can suppress local textile industries and contribute to the development of a reliance on other countries.

The solution is complex.

Donating your clothes can have both positive and negative effects. It's up to each of us to weigh the pros and cons and make an informed decision. Remember, every little bit helps! So, whether you decide to donate your clothes or find another way to reduce textile waste, every effort counts!

Here are three steps you can follow to minimize your clothing's impact on the environment:

- **Reduce your clothing purchases** and consider the ecological footprint of the textiles we consume. Donating clothing is a better alternative to throwing it away, but it doesn't entirely eliminate the impact of our clothing habits.

- **Opt for secondhand clothes** whenever possible. You can find used garments at local thrift stores or through online marketplaces.

- When buying new items, look for those made with **"recycled textiles"** to support the demand. This, in turn, motivates companies to close the loop and give new life to used garments.

SOLUTIONS

What to do with your old clothes?

One of the first reflexes we may have when we want to get rid of old clothes is to throw them away because, over the years, the society of (over)consumption has shaped us that way.

However, there are many more responsible options for getting rid of unwanted clothes that have become too big, too small, or too worn out!

Option 1: Relook

A dress becomes a skirt, a top becomes a hair accessory... often less complicated than we think, a simple pair of scissors and a bit of imagination (or a google search) can literally give a new life to a garment and avoid the trash!

Option 2: Offer

It is not uncommon for our loved ones to envy certain pieces of our wardrobe... Offering one of our clothes can be an excellent way to part with it, while making a nice gift.

Option 3: Exchange

More and more widespread, the "dressings exchanges" are easily organized between friends, the ideal way to have a good time and give a blow of freshness of clothing! Everybody wins: get rid of old pieces and find new items 100% second-hand!

Option 4: Sell

Dedicated events, specialized stores, websites, or mobile apps, today, there are many ways to sell your clothes! A financially interesting alternative and always much better than the trash can!

Option 5: Give back

The "return" option may be less known and widespread

than the others, but it is nevertheless well practiced by certain brands that offer to recover your old clothes and recycle or redesign them!

Option 6: Donate

Many associations and humanitarian organizations collect and redistribute clothes to people who need them.

The donation of clothing is a lovely alternative, purely altruistic, which brings great help to the neediest among us while offering a second life to our clothes.

If you decide to donate your clothes, don't wait too long to make sure your items are still wanted and in good shape.

However, be careful to choose the organization to which you turn. Unfortunately, some are not really ethical and do not really honor their commitments (we share more information in the previous questions).

So? Still, tempted by the trash can?

What is sustainable packaging?

Packaging is an essential part of protecting and delivering products, but it's also one of the biggest contributors to environmental waste.

Unfortunately, many brands still use excessive and over-the-top packaging that's not only harmful to the environment but also absurd.

That's why eco-conscious brands are taking action by reducing their use of packaging and opting for sustainable alternatives. They understand that packaging is a necessity, especially during transportation, but they strive to make it as environmentally friendly as possible.

Sustainable packaging comes in various forms and is always better for the environment. Whether made from recycled materials, biodegradable vegetable fibers or designed for multiple uses, there are many options available for brands to choose from.

Going a step further, some brands even choose to use vegetable ink and glue to create completely biodegradable packaging, which further reduces their carbon footprint.

In conclusion, the future of packaging is bright, and sustainable packaging offers a responsible alternative to traditional packaging that helps protect our planet.

Washing | How to take care of your clothes in an ethical way?

If we're going to write a book on ethical fashion, we might as well do it properly and dedicate a question to the washing and care of your clothes, because even at this stage, it is possible to adopt simple eco-responsible gestures... and yet they make all the difference!

Avoid over-washing

(because yes, it is possible to wear your clothes more than once before washing them again... and no, it's not dirty... it really isn't).

Indeed, not washing your clothes unnecessarily saves water, energy... and prolongs the life of your clothes which will wear out less quickly than when they are washed after being worn one day. (obviously, with the exception of underwear... please wash your underwear... and of course, after workouts, because, well you know, sweat)

Wash in cold water

For our every day, lightly soiled clothes, washing in cold water is more than enough to clean our clothes and uses much less energy than washing at high temperatures

Choose natural or eco-responsible detergents

Indeed, when rinsing clothes, all the ultra-polluting (and often perfectly useless) chemicals and detergents used are thrown directly into the waterways and represent a danger for all the micro-organisms that live there.

Use a wash bag for synthetic fiber clothing

During the various wash and rinse cycles, many microplastics from the clothing fibers "break off" and are released directly into the water and oceans. The simple use of a wash bag helps to avoid this problem. By using a filter in your washing machine, you can cut down the release of microfibers by a significant 80%[1].

Opt for air drying rather than machine drying

for obvious energy-saving reasons.

Try washing your clothes by hand

(sometimes it's much faster when there are few clothes to wash) and it's a real water and energy saver!

Choose energy-efficient washing machines

Far from being greenwashing, they really save water, energy... (and therefore money by the way!)

So, what did we learn about taking care of our clothes in an eco-friendly way?

Well, first of all, let's embrace the idea of re-wearing our clothes and say goodbye to over-washing. And when it's finally time for a wash, let's go for cold water and choose natural or eco-responsible detergents. Say hello to wash bags for our synthetic fiber clothing and goodbye to microplastics in the ocean. Air drying is the way to go, and hand washing is not only a water and energy saver but it's also a great workout for our arms. Finally, let's invest in an energy-efficient washing machine; not only will it save the planet, but it will also save us some green!

Who says being green is "not washing"?

Let's show the world that being eco-friendly is always in style!

How to find a responsible wedding dress?

Listen up, lovebirds! It's time to talk about wedding dresses.

Sure, they're beautiful and make you feel like royalty on your big day, but let's face it, wearing a dress just once is a bit of a waste, isn't it? Especially in today's world, where we're all about ethical consumption and sustainability.

I mean, think about it. Ethical fashion (just like a wedding) isn't just about looking fabulous, it's about making responsible choices. We need to move away from "single-use" clothes that just encourage overconsumption and waste. But how can you rock an amazing dress without contributing to the problem?

Well, there are options! Sure, you could go for ethical brands, secondhand options, or vintage dresses (all great choices, by the way), but what if I told you there's an even more ethical solution? What if you could rent your dream dress and save the planet while you're at it?

Think about it. You get to have an amazing wedding day in a dress that aligns with your values without feeling guilty about the impact it has on the environment and society. It's a win-win, folks!

So, don't let the pressure to own things get in the way of your special day. Take the sustainable route and rent your wedding dress.

Trust me, you'll be doing the world a favor and looking amazing while you're at it.

Is buying a Halloween costume ethical?

Halloween is the one day of the year when you can be whoever or whatever you want. It's the perfect opportunity to unleash your creativity and show off your spooky side.

But, let's face it, traditional Halloween costumes are not exactly ethical or eco-friendly. Buying a cheap, one-time-use costume is basically like buying fast fashion. You're supporting poor working conditions and contributing to waste and pollution.

But fear not, my ethically-conscious friends, because we've got some tips for making your Halloween costume a little more responsible.

First off, get creative! Halloween is all about using your imagination, so why not make your costume yourself? Not only is it way more eco-friendly, but it's also a chance to show off your crafting skills. You can transform old clothes or even an old costume into something new and exciting. Get out the sewing kit, add some accessories, and voila! You've got a one-of-a-kind costume that you can feel good about.

Tear a pair of pants apart, make holes in your shirt and put some ketchup on it! There you go! You can now be a zombie! Make it even more ethical by being a Vegan zombie!

So, don't let your Halloween costume haunt you with guilt. Put your creative cap on and make something unique and ethical. You'll look great and feel great knowing that you're doing your part to help the planet.

What if unisex fashion was the solution?

One of the major scourge of fast fashion today for the environment are the quantities of production! (not to mention the chemicals used, the respect of the workers, and the animal welfare, of course).

Always more, always faster. Always more choices, sizes, colors, versions, everything!

In a totally eco-centric approach, projecting ourselves in a unisex fashion more present in our stores, with a little less "gender-specific" choices, and coming back to more basic unisex pieces would allow us to limit the overproduction and the waste of clothes that end up in the trash without having ever been bought, to make room for other collections, other choices, other everything...

While it may sound utopian, fashion industry that prioritizes unisex clothing could make a difference.

What are the alternatives to animal "products"?

Firstly, any fabric that doesn't contain animal in it is an alternative to animal "products". It is vital to change our fashion perspective and realize that leather or vegan leather might not be the perfect solution.

Organic cotton, hemp, linen... All these fabrics are valid alternatives as well. It is better for the planet, the animals, and yourself.

Secondly, many alternatives are coming up every year. By the time you read this book, a new one might have come out! So take time to do your research and find the perfect one for you.

Material Innovation Initiative (MII), a nonprofit organization dedicated to advancing sustainable, animal-free materials as alternatives to traditional products like leather, wool, silk, down, and fur by focusing on research, knowledge sharing, and fostering connections to develop environmentally friendly materials, shared on their website a list of around 150 different innovative, and sustainable materials[1]. It exists as well many more alternatives created by independent designers, such as upcycled products that are not on this list.

If you thought there were not enough options, well, think twice.

Leather/Exotic leather

You wouldn't believe me if I told you that exist many alternatives to leather made of cactus, grapes, apples, tomatoes, banana, leaves, cork, trees, corn, mango, paper, synthetic, upcycled aluminum, coconut, coffee, kombucha, upcycled bubble wrap, recycled rubber, mushrooms... the list is pretty impressive.

These alternatives are often blended with synthetic to make the fabric more resistant and flexible (just like many genuine leathers). However, new technologies are rising, and by the time I am writing this book, I have talked to many engineers creating alternatives that will be 100% biodegradable!

Wool

This one is easy: wool can be replaced by any organic fabric such as cotton, bamboo, Tencel, hemp, or even recycled plastic fiber. Numerous wool alternatives that are indistinguishable from wool itself are available.

Down and feather

Just like wool, down is easily replaceable in the fashion industry, from recycled plastic (making it water resistant) to organic materials (making it sustainable). A company created a very innovative and eco-friendly alternative with a combination of wildflowers and a biopolymer made of corn and sugar cane. Many synthetic feathers are also available, making it a better choice for the animals.

Fur and silk

The search for alternatives to fur and silk has led to remarkable innovations. Biofabricated furs and silks, made through advanced scientific processes, offer the same luxurious feel without ethical concerns. Similarly, plant-based materials are being developed to mimic the texture and warmth of fur, and regenerated fibers offer a silk-like experience that's both sustainable and cruelty-free... and fully biodegradable and compostable!

As we continue to explore and develop new materials, the possibilities for sustainable and ethical alternatives seem endless. The industry is in a constant state of innovation, with new materials being introduced regularly.

This dynamic landscape not only provides more choices for consumers but also fosters a more sustainable approach to production and consumption.

The array of alternatives to animal products is a testament to human creativity and our growing commitment to sustainability. As we move forward, these materials are not just replacing their animal-based counterparts; they are setting new standards for quality, ethics, and environmental responsibility. With ongoing research and development, the future of materials looks bright, promising a world where fashion and sustainability coexist harmoniously.

This book isn't just bad news, after all.

If you need more profound research on all the available fabrics, please check our source at the end of this book. Listing all the alternatives would be too lengthy and soon become outdated, as new vegan options are created every year.

How to really support vegan and ethical brands? (even for free)

Well, is there any need to introduce this answer by explaining why it is good to support or be interested in ethical and vegan alternatives?

So, to support and encourage these alternatives, obviously, the first action to take, is to buy from brands that offer ethical and vegan products.

But without entering into a logic of overconsumption (even if it is about healthy products), it is also possible to act and support responsible brands without buying anything.

How do you do it? **By spreading their message, their products, and their values.** And how do you do that? By following their content on the internet, by sharing their content on social networks, by discussing with your friends and family about them, etc.

Ethical and vegan fashions deserve greater visibility to sensitize as many people as possible.

Why seek to raise awareness among as many people as possible? Because it is one of the major keys to activating a fundamental change in consumption habits.

Indeed, most customers continue to consume harmful products simply because they don't even know they are harmful.

To make things change, it doesn't take much... communication is the key! Because yes... **a tiny action can have a huge impact!**

How can we be sure that a brand is truly ethical?

When shopping for ethical products, look for brands that follow the five key commitments of the "**HEART**" principles:

H - Health & Happiness: An ethical brand knows that happy workers make for happy customers. That's why they make sure their workers are treated with respect and dignity, working in safe and healthy conditions and earning a fair wage. No child labor allowed!

E - Environmentally Responsible: A brand that's serious about ethics is serious about the environment. That means they're doing their part to reduce their carbon footprint, steer clear of harmful chemicals, and take other steps to be gentle on Mother Nature.

A - Animal Kindness: A brand that's all about ethics knows that all creatures, big and small, deserve to be treated with kindness. That's why they avoid any form of exploitation, animal "products" or testing on animals. They believe in creating products that are cruelty-free and kind to all creatures, great and small!

R - Reasonable & Fair: When it comes to price, an ethical brand strikes a balance. They want to make sure their workers are paid fairly for their hard work, but they also don't want to overcharge you for their products. It's all about finding the sweet spot!

T - True & Trustworthy (or Transparency): Ethical brands prioritize honesty and transparency in all their dealings. They are open about their manufacturing processes, sourcing of materials, and business practices.

Ethical brands believe in building trust with their customers by being forthcoming about how their products are made, where they come from, and who is involved in the making.

This transparency ensures that consumers can make informed decisions, trusting that they are supporting a brand that aligns with their values and ethics. These brands don't just talk the talk; they walk the walk, demonstrating their commitment to ethical practices in every aspect of their operations.

By following these HEART principles, ethical brands proves that they are true to their values and trustworthy in their commitments.

Shop with confidence, knowing that the brands and products you support are making a positive impact on the world.

Consumers or brands, who has the power?

Spoiler alert: it's us! The consumers! We have the power!

How do you do it?

By choosing what to buy or not to buy! Because we (and especially our money) are the real interest, the real purpose of all this, of all these production chains, of all these creation processes that suffocate the planet, the workers, and the animals.

So, if we choose to change the game, to reverse the trend, by focusing our efforts on showing our desires... we can change things... we have the power over the brands, which will "bend" to our wishes, to the willingness of the market.

(Spoiler alert number 2)

Brands will go where our desire goes, where the purchasing power goes.

How to do it?

To reverse the trend, to express our desires? Simply by realizing that "buying is voting" - finally take back the power over what we buy, without falling into the wheels of fast fashion that create needs we do not have and by choosing to consume responsibly, ethically, vegan, ecologically!

#ToBuyIsToVote

Is vegan fashion just a passing trend?

It is indeed quite the opposite.

By definition, a "trend' is a general direction in which something tends to move, change or develop. Trends could be ephemeral and disappear as fast as they got famous, and they can keep coming back and forth, but in the idea, there will always be new trends to replace the old current ones.

The vegan fashion textiles, accessories, and clothing market has been solidly established and in full expansion since several years ago.

In fact, we can notice an absolute explosion of new brands proposing vegan products or choosing to dedicate themselves totally to vegan fashion, thus revolutionizing our consumption. Even some of the most controversial fast fashion brands are introducing vegan items and alternatives in their collections. #ChangeIsNow

Much more than a passing trend, vegan fashion, respectful of the environment and animal welfare, is a true lifestyle, a way of thinking towards tomorrow.

Vegan fashion is the choice to act today on a daily basis for a healthier and more respectful future to pass on to future generations; The choice to act today, take part in the revolution, and be a leader of a life-saving movement, or the choice to join it in a few years, later, along with everyone else.

**Vegan Fashion is not a trend,
it is a REVOLUTION.**

Is 3D design a good solution?

Let's make it clear and straightforward: **YES**, 3D designs are definitely shaking things up in the fashion world, making it more sustainable.

3D designs allow designers to create and modify garments in a digital environment before any fabric is cut or sewn. This means that the entire design process can be completed without producing a single physical prototype, from conceptualization to the final approval of patterns.

3D design drastically reduces the waste generated during the prototyping phase by eliminating the need for multiple physical samples! This shift could significantly lower the environmental footprint of fashion production.

Designers can also test fits, fabrics, and styles in a virtual environment, identifying and correcting issues without the time and resources required for traditional sampling. This speeds up the design process and reduces the materials and energy consumed in creating garments.

The future is bright for the sustainable fashion movement!

Can you imagine virtual showrooms and digital fittings to offer consumers a new way to engage with fashion, reducing the need for physical samples and potentially slowing the fast fashion cycle?

No more ordering an item online that doesn't fit you, then shipping it back and exchanging it repeatedly, creating more shipping and pollution.

In a world where overproduction and overconsumption are significant issues, the ability to visualize and customize clothing virtually before anything is produced could lead to more thoughtful and sustainable purchasing decisions.

However, it is essential to acknowledge that 3D design wouldn't be enough on its own for all the sustainability challenges facing the fashion industry.

While it offers significant advantages regarding waste reduction and efficiency, the sustainability of 3D design also depends on how it is implemented.

For example, if you create a 3D model but decide to use unethical practices or harmful fabric to produce it, it won't be sustainable.

FACT

Creating a 3D model opens up exciting possibilities for sustainability
IF
this innovation is coupled with ethical practices and eco-friendly materials in production.

And now?

Okay, everyone, let's take a moment here and flip the script on feeling blue and thinking the world's gone bonkers.

It's time to wipe away those tears and give yourself a TED talk: "No way I am adding to this mess! I'm starting with small steps for a big change!"

Seriously, look for a mirror, gaze into your eyes (See the determination?) and pinky promise yourself. It's a simple way to commit to your goal, like a silent vow to be part of the solution, not the problem.

This book has not just been a collection of pages but a journey towards understanding the impact of our choices. It is a call to adopt ethical fashion practices, to rethink our consumption habits, and to embrace sustainability not as a trend, but as a lifestyle.

Remember, it's not about overhauling your life overnight. Start with small, manageable steps. Whether it's choosing to buy from responsible brands, learning to upcycle, or simply educating others about the importance of sustainable practices, every action counts.

Remind yourself that change begins with a single step. The road ahead may be long and filled with challenges, but it's a path worth taking. Along the way, you'll find a community of like-minded individuals, each contributing in their own way to a more sustainable and just world.

Let's not underestimate the power of individual actions. Together, we add up to a wave of change, capable of transforming the industry and, ultimately, the world.

So, take a deep breath, step forward with purpose, and embrace the journey ahead. Your choices have power. Use them to weave a better future, one garment at a time.

Remember, this is not the end but a new beginning. A chance to redefine fashion, to make it kinder to the planet and its inhabitants. So, let's roll up our sleeves and get to work. There's a whole world out there waiting to be inspired by what you do next.

Let's get started!

FACT

> **Never forget that even the smallest actions can make a BIG difference in the world.**

A good place to start.

As we turn the final page of this journey, I'd like to extend my heartfelt gratitude for your companionship through these pages. Together, we've explored the nuanced and critical facets of ethical fashion, uncovering truths and challenging misconceptions along the way. But the conversation doesn't end here; it's merely the beginning.

A good place to start is by recognizing the power each of us holds in shaping a more ethical and sustainable future for fashion. You can play a pivotal role in this movement, and here are a few ways to do so:

Leave a Review: Share your thoughts on this book by leaving a review. Your insights not only contribute to the conversation but also encourage others to embark on this enlightening journey towards ethical fashion, and will encourage me to keep spreading awarnesss the right way!

Spread the Word: Talk about the insights you've gained with friends, family, and on your social media platforms. The more we discuss these issues, the greater our collective impact can be. You can literally just take a picture of the page that resonated the most with you and share it!

Engage Online: Visit fakemovement.com to dive deeper into the world of vegan and ethical fashion. Here, you'll find a wealth of resources, including podcasts, a vegan and ethical fashion marketplace, and blog articles, to further your education and involvement.

Subscribe to Our Newsletter: Stay connected and informed by subscribing to our newsletter. You'll receive the latest updates, tips, and events related to ethical fashion, keeping you at the forefront of this important movement.

Send me an Email: Use the 'contact us' feature on fakemovement.com or directly email me at info@fakemovement.com. I would love to learn what you liked or disliked about this book and how you think I/we can push the boundaries on elevating sustainable fashion. I can't wait to read your feedback!

Together, we can ensure that this book reaches the hands of many, spreading awareness and igniting change. Your actions, no matter how small they may seem, play a part in a domino effect, leading to a world where fashion is not only about style but also about sustainability and ethics.

Thank you for joining me on this journey. Let's continue to learn, share, and advocate for a future where fashion respects the planet and all beings.

FAKEMOVEMENT.COM

THANK YOU

A special "Thank you" to Sucely Montoya, Julie Dubos, and Georgina Servin for helping me making this book readable.

Thank you to the F.A.K.E. community for always being here and supporting ethical fashion.

Thank YOU! The person holding this book for reading this and being a part of the change!

SOURCES

WHAT IS FASHION?

What is Fashion, and who created it?

1- Nicola Davis, "Scientists find evidence of humans making clothes 120,000 years ago" in the Guardian, Online: https://www.theguardian.com/science/2021/sep/16/scientists-find-evidence-of-humans-making-clothes-120000-years-ago (Sep 16, 2021)

2- Jacqueline C. Kent, Business Builders in Fashion - Charles Frederick Worth - The Father of Haute Couture, Oliver Press (2003)

What is Sustainable Fashion?

1- Report of the World Commission on Environment and Development - Our Common Future, United Nations (October 1987)

What is Vegan Fashion?

1- Pulse of the Fashion industry - Global Fashion Agenda (2017)

What is Greenwashing?

1- The "Six Sins of Greenwashing" - TerraChoice Environmental Marketing Inc (2007)

TEXTILE and its environmental impact

Cotton or Organic cotton, what's the difference?

1- International Cotton Advisory Committee. (2021, June). ICAC cotton data book 2021.

2- The green, blue, and grey water footprint of crops and derived crop products - M. M. Mekonnen and A. Y. Hoekstra (May 25, 2011)

3 - Life Cycle Assessment (LCA) or Organic Cotton - Textile Exchange (November 2014)

4- Get the facts about Organic Cotton - Organic Trade Association (OTA), June 2022.

5- EJF, 2007, The Deadly Chemicals in Cotton, Environmental Justice Foundation in collaboration with Pesticide Action Network UK, London.

Is bamboo fabric ecological?

1- Carbon sequestration and carbon emissions reduction through bamboo forests and products - INBAR - International Bamboo and Rattan Organisation (2018)

2- Textile Fiber Products Identification Act - Federal Trade Commission.

Is hemp the solution of tomorrow?

1- Global water footprint of industrial hemp textile - J. Averink - September 2015

2- International Cotton Advisory Committee. (2021, June). ICAC cotton data book 2021.

3- Advances in the Performance and Application of Hemp Fiber - Hongjie Zhang (2018)

Is Linen the solution of tomorrow?

1- Life Cycle Assessment (LCA) of European flax scutched fiber - CELC European Confederation of Flax and Hemp (February 2022)

Fabrics: Which one has the worst environmental impact?

1- Pulse of the Fashion industry - Global Fashion Agenda (2017)

ANIMALS in fashion

Chemicals - Which ones are used to create leather?

1- Chromium released from leather – I: exposure conditions that govern the release of chromium(III) and chromium(VI) - Wiley-Blackwell (February 3rd, 2015)

2- The Toxic Price of Leather - Sean Gallagher (March 5th, 2014)

3- Future Fashion White Papers - Earth Pledge Foundation, edited by Leslie Hoffman (March 17, 2017)

4- Cuir: les forçats de la mode - les ravages de la mondialisation - Nicolas Daniel - (Novembre 14th, 2020)

5- Chemicals Used in Leather Processing - International School of Tanning Technology (ISTT) https://sites.google.com/site/isttschool/useful-information/chemicals-used-in-leather-processing

What is Chromium?

1- Chromium released from leather – I: exposure conditions that govern the release of chromium(III) and chromium(VI) - Wiley-Blackwell (February 3rd, 2015)

2- The Toxic Price of Leather - Sean Gallagher (March 5th, 2014)

3- Benefits and problems of chrome tanning in leather processing: Approach a greener technology in leather industry - Maraz KM. - 2021

Is vegetable tanning/veg-tan if animal leather an ethical and ecological solution?

1- Measuring the Environmental Footprint of Leather Processing Technologies - Rafael Laurenti - 14 October 2016

Pee in leather?

1- Suetonius, Vespasian 23. Cf. Dio Cassius, Roman History, bk. 65, ch. 14.5

1- "The journal of urology" - Vol. 183, No. 4 - 1133 - May 31th 2010

2- "From Gunpowder to Teeth Whitener: The Science Behind Historic Uses of Urine" - Smithsonian - Mohi Kumar - August 20th, 2013

3- "Fashionable pee: cleaning, dyeing, and tanning" - Mediamatic.net - Anna Piccoli - July 25th, 2015

Plastic in leather?

1- Species Identification - F.A.K.E. movement - University of Cincinnati - Leather Research Laboratory (March 21st, 2022)

Cat and dog leather… does it really exist?

1- "The American Journal of Physical Anthropology" - Raul Tito - University of Oklahoma

2- Dog Slaughtered for Leather - PETA undercover investigation (November, 2014) https://investigations.peta.org/china-dog-leather/

3- DNA for Species Identification in Leather: Fraud detection and endangered species protection - Maxime Merheb - September 2015

4- 19 U.S. Code § 1308 - Prohibition on importation of dog and cat fur products

5- Species Identification - F.A.K.E. movement - University of Cincinnati - Leather Research Laboratory (March 21st, 2022)

6- "China Bans The Selling of Dog and Cat Meat" - Four Paws - May 25th, 2020.

Kangaroo leather?

1- Kangaroo: A Love-Hate Story - Kate Clere McIntyre, Michael McIntyre (January 19th, 2018)

2- A Shot in the Dark - A Report on Kangaroo Harvesting - Dror Ben-Ami (2019)

Exotic leather, how luxurious it is?

1- Exposed: Crocodiles and Alligators Factory-Farmed for Hermès 'Luxury' Goods - PETA investigation (2009)

Human leather… Really?

1- former website Humanleather.co.uk

2- https://www.tinagorjanc.com/pure-human - Pure Human - Tina Gorjanc (June 2016)

Is wool ethical?

1- 14 PETA Wool Industry Exposés on 117 Farms in Six Countries. Enough Is Enough! You Can Help. - PETA (People for the Ethical Treatment of Animals) - December 1st, 2020
https://investigations.peta.org/victoria-australia-wool-expose/

2- Australian Wool Exchange – AWEX (2021) Static auction mulesing status statistics by micron.

3- Revealed: government knew of farm poisoning risk but failed to act - the guardian - Tom Levitt (April 20th, 2015)

Alpaca fiber, is it ethical?

1- Groundbreaking Undercover Investigation: Crying, Vomiting Alpacas Tied Down, Cut Up for Sweaters and Scarves - PETA (May 31st, 2020)

2- Water for food - the continuing debate - Wayne Meyer (January 2004)

What is cashmere? Is it ethical?

1- "How conscious is cashmere? The ethical options to wear this winter" - Evening Standard - Karen Dacre (November 20th, 2018)

2- "How your cashmere sweater is decimating Mongolia's grasslands" - NPR - Rob Schmitz (December 9th, 2016)

3- "Breaking PETA Exposé Reveals Cruelty in Your Cashmere Sweater" - PETA investigation (2019)

4- "PETA Exposé Reveals Cruelty Behind Your Cashmere Sweater" - Youtube video - PETA (May 13th, 2019)

5- "How sustainable cashmere is reversing land degradation in Mongolia" - United Nations Development Programme - (June 15, 2021)

Rats in my clothes?

1- Rat fur found in Chinese-made cashmere coats - ANSA - Agenzia Nazionale Stampa Associata (February 3rd, 2014)

Down, is it ethical?

1- Exposed: Despite 'Responsible Down Standards,' Farms Still Live-Plucking Geese - PETA (2012)

Why silk is so bad for the planet?

1- Neuronal localisation of immunoreactive enkephalin and β-endorphin in the earthworm - J.ALUMETS, R. HÅKANSON, F. SUNDLER & J. THORELL (June 28th, 1979)

2- How silk is made? A step by step guide - Biddle Sawyer Silks (August 29th, 2020)

Are pearls ethical?

1- What are you wearing around your neck? Here's why you shouldn't wear pearls - PETA (Rebecca Maness) - November 30th, 2022

Fur will soon be banned worldwide, why not leather?

1- "Undercover investigation on six fox farms in Finland revealed suffering of countless animal" - Youtube - Fur Free Alliance - 2023

1- "EXPOSED: Undercover investigation at fur farm shows the lives behind the label" - The Humane Society - August 31, 2020

1- "PETA investigation Uncovers Cruelty on Chinchilla Fur Farm" - PETA - 2005

2- Toxic Fur - Dutch report of the research laboratory Bremer Umweltinstitut - Bont Voor Dieren - 2015

2- Poisons in Furs - Study by EcoAid commissioned by Four Paws - 2011

2- Toxic Fur: The impacts of fur production on the environment and the risks to human health - The humane society - Januar 29th, 2009

3- Toxic Fur: A Global Issue - Prof Jacob de Boer - ACT Asia - 2018

4- Toxic Fur - Fur Free Alliance - http://www.furfreealliance.com/toxic-fur

5- Ecopel - https://www.ecopel.com

6- "Natural mink fur and faux fur products, an environmental comparison" - Marijn Bijleveld - June 2013

HUMANS in fashion

What is a "Sweatshop"?

1- United States General Accounting Office. "Sweatshops in the U.S: Opinions on Their Extent and Possible Enforcement Options." GAO, 1988. Web Accessed February 19, 2014

What is "Rana Plaza' and what happened there?

1- "Why do we need a Fashion Revolution?" - fashionrevolution.org

1- "The True Cost" - Documentary - 2015

Is the "minimum wage" ethical?

1- "Minimum Wage Level for Garment Workers in the World" - Sheng lu - Dec 4, 2020

2- "The International Labour Organization and the Living Wage: A Historical Perspective" - Emmanuel Reynaud - 2017

3- "Living Wage" - Labour Behind the Label.

"The fashion industry exploits children", is it true?

1- "Global Estimates of Child Labour" - ILO (International Labour Organization) - 2012/2016

What is MICA? And why is it so bad?

1- The Dark Secret Behind Your Favorite Makeup Products - Shady - Refinery29 - May 4th, 2019

Is it possible to be a feminist and buy fast fashion?

1- "How to achieve gender equality in global garment supply chains" - ILO (International Labour Organization)

1- ILOSTAT explorer website (ilo.org) - International Labour Organization

3- "Gender pay gaps in the garment, textile and footwear sector in developing Asia" - ILO (International Labour Organization) - 20 December 2018

4- "Moving the Needle: Gender equality and decent work in Asia's garment sector" - ILO (International Labour Organization) - 5 May 2021

5- "Sexual Harassment in the Workplace: Does it Affect Firm Performance and Profits?" Xirong Lin, Laura Babbitt, Drusilla Brown. Better Work Discussion Paper No. 16. ILO, Geneva. November 2014.

6- "Myanmar's women face routine pregnancy tests and sexual harassment in sweatshops" - Libby Hogan - ABC.net - 14 April 2018

What diseases "toxic" clothing can cause?

1- "Identification of non-regulated aromatic amines of toxicological concern which can be cleaved from azo dyes used in clothing textiles" - 2024, July - National Library Of Medicine.

2- "Formaldehyde" - December 5th, 2022 - National Cancer Institute.

Does buying new clothes make us happy?

1- The Easterlin Paradox - The National Archives (website).

2- "Why Instant Gratification Isn't So Gratifying" -September 19, 2017 - Pamela N. Danziger - Forbes.

Could fashion have an impact on our mental health?

1- Mind what you wear, psychology of fashion - Professor Karen Pine - May 13th, 2014

2- Journal of Experimental Social Psychology - Volume 48, issue 4 - Hajo Adam & Adam D. Galinsky - July 2012

PRODUCTION and its environmental impact

How many clothes are made each year?

1- "The true cost" - Andrew Morgan - 2015

1- "Our love of cheap clothing has a hidden cost – it's time for a fashion revolution" - World Economic Forum - April 22, 2016

1- " Fashion has a misinformation problem. That's bad for the environment." - Alden Wicker - Han 31, 2020

1- "Style that's sustainable: A new fast-fashion formula" - Nathalie Remy, Eveline Speelman, Steven Swartz - Mckinsey report - October 20, 2016

2- The fashion transparency index 2023 - Fashion Revolution - July 12, 2023

3- Ellen MacArthur Foundation, A new textiles economy: Redesigning fashion's future, (2017, http://www.ellenmacarthurfoundation.org/publications).

4- "Preferred Fiber & Materials Market Report" - Textile Exchange - October 2022

4- Ellen MacArthur Foundation, A new textiles economy: Redesigning fashion's future, (2017, http://www.ellenmacarthurfoundation.org/publications).

5- Pulse of the Fashion industry - Global Fashion Agenda (2017)

Is 'made in Europe' or 'made in USA' necessarily ethical?

1- Unfit wages: US department of Labor survey finds widespread violations by southern California garment industry contractors, manufacturers - Wage and Hour Division - March 22, 2023

What happens to unsold clothes?

1- "Burberry burns bags, clothes and perfume worth millions" - BBC - July 19th, 2018

2- "Explainer: Why fast fashion brands destroy unsold clothes" - Eco-Business

Microplastic, how much is released into the oceans by the fashion industry?

1- Boucher, J. and Friot D. (2017). Primary Microplastics in the Oceans: A Global Evaluation of Sources. Gland, Switzerland: IUCN. 43pp.

2- Sherrington, 2016; Ellen MacArthur Foundation, 2017

3- Plastic in textiles: towards a circular economy for synthetic textiles in Europe - EEA European Environment Agency - January 28th 2021

4- Engineering out fashion waste - Institution of Mechanical Engineers - September 2018

5- Potential microplastic release from the maritime industry: Abrasion of rope - International Marine Litter Research Unit, University of Plymouth - September 1st 2021

6- "The efficiency of devices intended to reduce microfibre release during clothes washing" - Science of the Total Environment, Volume 738 - October 10th 2020.

Water, how much is wasted by the fashion industry?

1- Niinimäki, K., Peters, G., Dahlbo, H. et al. The environmental price of fast fashion. Nat Rev Earth Environ 1, 189–200 (2020). https://doi.org/10.1038/s43017-020-0039-9

Is it ethical to donate your clothes?

1- American Apparel and Footwear Association, International Trade Commission, the U.S. Department of Commerce's Office of Textiles and Apparel, and the Council for Textile Recycling.

2- SMART Secondary Materials And Recycled Textiles - faq "How are textiles recycled?"

3- Textiles: Material-Specific Data - EPA United States Environmental Protection Agency - "Fact and Figures about Materials, Waste and Recycling" - 2018

4- "Facilitating a Circular Economy for Textiles" Workshop Report - NIST (National Institute of Standards and Technology) - Kelsea Schumacher, Amanda L. Forster - May 09, 2022

5- "Fast Fashion Is Creating an Environmental Crisis" - Newsweek Magazine - Alden Wicker - September 1st, 2016

6- "Textile Waste Facts" Panel - Textiles waste, Environmental Justice, and the Aftermath of Fashion - Make Fashion Clen (MFC) - Matilda Lartey - 2023

7- "Protectionist ban on imported used clothing" - UN.org - Africa Renewal, Franck Kuwonu - December 2017, March 2018

SOLUTIONS

Washing - how to take care of your clothes in an ethical way?

1- "The efficiency of devices intended to reduce microfibre release during clothes washing" - Science of the Total Environment, Volume 738 - October 10th 2020.

What are the alternatives to animal "products"?

1- Material Innovator Database - (MII) Material Innovation Initiative - https://materialinnovation.org/next-gen-innovation-databases/innovators-database/

Made in United States
North Haven, CT
22 May 2024